Chasing
the
California Dream

A Solo Horseback Journey
Along the California Coast

⁺ ⋆ ⁺

Lisa F. Wood

*May all your
dreams come true
Lisa F. Wood*

LOST〰
COAST
PRESS

Chasing the California Dream
A Solo Horseback Journey Along the California Coast
Copyright ©2001 by Lisa F. Wood

All rights reserved. This book may not be reproduced in whole or in part, by any means, electronic or mechanical, without prior written permission from the publisher. For information, or to order additional copies of this book, please contact:

Lost Coast Press
155 Cypress Street
Fort Bragg, CA 95437
(800) 773-7782
www.cypresshouse.com

Cover design and illustration:
Charles Hathaway / Mendocino Graphics

ISBN 1-882897-63-3   LCCN 2001-130427

Manufactured in the U.S.A.
First edition
2 4 6 8 9 7 5 3 1

With Heartfelt Thanks To –

My parents who helped and worried (more than usual)

∗ ∗ ∗

*My friends who encouraged me, especially
Catherine Dower, who spent countless hours
reviewing early versions of this text*

∗ ∗ ∗

The many strangers who showed kindness and hospitality

∗ ∗ ∗

And of course Cacho, who carried me so many miles

Dedicated to All Those Who Dream

Written in Memory of:

Michael Jory Langsford

and

Michael Joseph Bollard

Contents

Chasing
the
California
Dream

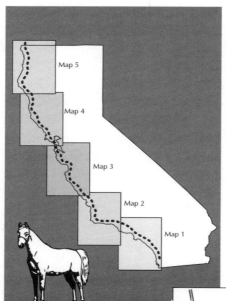

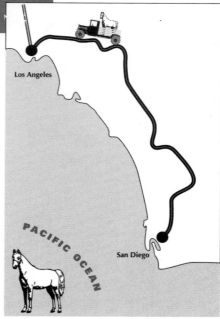

Map 1

1
Reaching for the Dream

Whatahen I dream, my subconscious twists the familiar into something new, often surreal, but also compelling, like swimming with whales and miraculously being able to breathe underwater, or flying low over rooftops, propelled by sheer willpower. So it was that I dreamed of traveling through California—on horseback.

A scene from a book called *California Coast Trails* formed the basis of my fantasy. The book described Joseph Smeaton Chase's journey along the coast of California in 1911, evoking in my mind an image of a man in a broad-brimmed hat riding a horse along a beach at sunset, a solitary figure, unhurried. In my dream, the lines of his silhouette shifted and became an outline of me in his place, riding relaxed, my motion fluid, behind me the setting sun glistening off the Pacific waves. I do not try to enact most of my dreams, but in this case common sense failed me.

I started doing unusual things to prepare, like browsing the classifieds in search of an antique saddle similar to the one used by J. Smeaton Chase (and I found the one I was looking for—a military saddle in the design credited to General McClellan). I sometimes found it difficult to explain what I was doing. For example, I went to a supply store and explained to the clerk why I needed an extra-heavy-duty rope latch. The woman standing in the checkout line behind me interrupted to ask, "Wait, let me get this straight, you're riding your horse from Southern California to Oregon?" I nodded. She asked if it wouldn't be easier to take my horse in a trailer.

The questions foremost in my mind were not the ones most often asked of me. The most frequently asked questions were things like, was I going to bring a gun (no), and, did I plan to go alone (no, my horse was coming with me). But the question that dominated my mind was whether I could make it. I was not alone in doubting my abilities, and to try and fail would bring resounding affirmation to my detractors. Of course, depending on the nature of my failure, embarrassment could be the least of my worries. My less dire but no less relentless question was what would I get out of it? One expects to obtain deep spiritual insight from such an endeavor. That puts the pressure on to find it.

I'd like to say I set off with sure, bold strides, following confidently in the hoofprints of Mr. Chase's horse. It was more like every nerve firing in uncontrolled panic, a feeling I hadn't experienced since I was eighteen years old. At that age, with all the profound wisdom of my teen years to go on, I decided it would be a really keen idea to go parachuting. I realized the error of my judgement only when actually faced with the daunting prospect of exiting the aircraft. Now, some fourteen years later, I found I hadn't learned my lesson. I was still putting myself into positions I felt ill equipped to handle.

As if I hadn't spent a year and a half planning, I suddenly found myself camped out with my horse, a small Appaloosa named Cacho, in the Santa Monica Mountains. I tossed and turned in my nylon sleeping bag, horrifically overwhelmed by my undertaking, feeling as if I was tumbling through the air. I peered out of the mosquito-proof mesh of my tent door at the shape of Cacho resting in the moonlight. Sleepless, I tried to figure a way to call it quits. Because I had taken an unpaid leave from work and rented out my house, there seemed nothing to do but at least give it a try. Exploring the vastness of my inadequacy, I consoled myself with the thought that I would always hereafter be able to win the award for the most unique and possibly ludicrous answer to the question: How did you spend your summer?

If I thought the enterprise was going to be comfortable, the weather on my first day out soon abused me of this notion. The temperature rose with the sun, hot and humid, with tall gray clouds closing in overhead. Sweat shone on Cacho's neck and my hat made a wet, circular imprint on my hair. To add to the experience, black biting flies the size of June bugs probed my skin and Cacho's hide. The inside of my knees blistered and developed open sores where the seam of my jeans pressed against the saddle. Any illusion of an attractive image was squelched by a serious nose-burn, despite my hat and repeated applications of sunscreen, and the subsequent glamorous peeling process.

To be evenhanded in my description, I should point out that, physical and emotional trauma notwithstanding, even that first frightening day had its highlights. Cacho carried me through spectacular scenery in the Santa Monica Mountains. Gnarled, rusty-red volcanic boulders peppered the tall canyon walls. Deep green vegetation clung tenaciously to all but the completely vertical rock faces. The clouds closed in and dropped a smattering of hot rain, then, exhausted with the effort of unity, broke again into individual thunderheads that thinned and eventually evaporated into the hot air. At a sycamore-shaded stream, just as I noted the pleasant view, Cacho picked up a stone in his hoof. I got off and picked it out. Swinging back into the saddle, I misjudged the extra oomph necessary to get my leg over the bedroll and nearly gave myself a hernia. So it was that I vacillated minute by minute from confidence and pleasure to fear and discomfort.

* * *

Three days later I discovered that my troubles had only just begun. The honeymoon of peaceful trails through the mountains ended abruptly at an intersection with Highway 1. Trucks sent my hat skittering off my head as they barreled past, the string cutting into my neck as it prevented me from losing this important piece of gear. The smell of exhaust fouled the moist marine air. Setting off camping with no experience and little but determination to see me through had been silly enough, but riding along the highway and into the urban area of Oxnard indicated the need for serious psychological evaluation.

Cacho sucked in his lips and swished his tail with annoyance at the noisy cars and the windblast from passing trucks. He had not been consulted about the advisability of the outing and, judging by his reaction to the traffic, surely would have voted against it. Once in town, however, the cars slowed and he seemed to resent them less. He clomped surprisingly readily down the concrete sidewalk past convenience stores, video rental shops, and Hallmark card shops, attracting more notice than a bulldozer at an Earth First convention. People yelled and children shrieked. Initially I blushed, complimented and a little embarrassed, but when the attention began to feel like an unrelenting assault, I began to understand why a celebrity might long for privacy.

As we neared a Taco Bell, the young women clerks saw us, pointed, and snickered. I was hungry and Cacho needed water, so I reined him into the drive-through, getting in line behind a car. By the time the car had pulled forward, the young clerks were so overcome with hysterical laughter at the sight of us that they couldn't talk. One of them put her head down on the counter and sobbed; the other covered her face with one hand and waved me up to the window with the other. When I got to the window, they kept a respectful distance, pulling their arms protectively toward their bodies, tittering nervously, but a bit more subdued.

Finally one of them managed to squeak out the words, "Did you want to order something?"

"I'd like a taco and a Dr. Pepper for me, and a large water, no ice, for my friend. And can we eat that in, um, the grassy area over there?" I asked, pointing. They filled my order and breathlessly invited Cacho to eat the lawn, and then returned to their convulsions.

I held a paper cup for him and he drank water like a person, with one lip below and one lip above the rim. I ate the taco quickly and continued down the road, drinking my Dr. Pepper as we walked, for the moment happy to be in town, and still chuckling to myself over the incident.

* * *

As much as I'd enjoyed the ridiculous situation at the Taco Bell, taking a horse through cities proved nerve-wracking. Three days later I heaved a sigh of relief and left the crowded coastal communities, heading into the mountains on a trail east of Santa Barbara. People I met had cautioned me about the route, saying a rockslide had made the trail impassible, advising me to ride through town instead. I disregarded the warnings for two reasons: I was sick of urban hazards, and I could not help trusting the one man who recommended the trail.

He was a tall man named Tony, with an earnest, weather-beaten face. His beard, dark with bits of gray, looked as if it was seldom if ever trimmed. His manner and his experience as a packer (he took people on pack trips on horses) gave me great confidence in his advice. Tony said that if Cacho were sure-footed I should be able to make it.

To make the trip a little easier for Cacho, Tony said he would meet me at the top of the grade and bring my tent and sleeping bag. He repacked for me, tying the legs of a pair of his long jeans and using them as a wither bag to move some of the weight further forward.

The trail began as a wide and well-maintained thoroughfare, which I saw as a sign that I had made the right decision. I cheerfully greeted a few other hikers and equestrians enjoying the shade under a broad, thick canopy of oaks and sycamores. The company dwindled, however, as the trail thinned and became more heavily festooned with poison oak, until at last Cacho and I trundled on in solitude.

Stepping through some inviting dust, Cacho took me by surprise, managing to get down for a roll before I could kick him up. I stood to the side while he rolled with the saddle and packs on. "Naughty boy," I scolded, and he pretended not to understand. He staggered to his feet with a grunt and tried to look very innocent. He shook vigorously, making the gear thunder and the dust fly.

As we continued, the trail became even worse. Cacho scrambled over rocks and finally, where the trail disappeared altogether, he carried me onto a loose, gravelly landslide. Above the talus a tree grew sideways from a big boulder, and below the slide the trunks of trees were half-buried in rubble. Below the trees the jumble disappeared in a sheer rocky drop to the gorge below. Cacho maintained his footing until he was well into the rockslide. Then for some reason the gear slipped, or the substrate shifted, or possibly he spooked. Anyway, he lost his footing and reeled backward.

On a scale of one to ten, I have a bravery quotient of approximately minus five, and thus reflexively set about saving my own skin. I jumped from the saddle on the up-hill side, landing in the crumbling scree and sliding under Cacho. In what seemed like a slow-motion movie scene, I saw Cacho's front hooves hovering dramatically in the air above me. There seemed no alternative but that they would crush my skull into the side of the mountain and I would die in that moment. Yet, I sensed somehow that Cacho would do all he could to prevent that from happening. He acted more like a somewhat grumpy guardian angel than like an unrelenting or even accidental angel of death.

His muscles could hold him in the rearing position only so long. As he came down he turned his head to look for me. The instant our eyes met he swerved toward the downhill side and avoided landing on me. In doing so he basically threw himself into the gorge. Finding nothing solid beneath him, he slid more than fifty feet down the scree until he came to a stop against a tree. His head was entangled in a branch, and bits of shale hid his legs up to his belly. Four feet beyond the tree, pieces of rock smacked noisily as they bounced their way to the bottom of the gorge.

He stood still, seeming to wait for instructions from me. I told him "Ho, buddy, I'll get you. Just stay steady." I tried to keep my voice calm. The seriousness of the situation had not yet dawned on me, so I was, in fact, calm, despite a nagging concern that he might have pulled or broken something while struggling against the shale.

I slid down the hot, jagged gravel. Feet-first on my belly, I barely managed to stop before I crashed into him. So much debris came down with me that I had to dig under it to reach the buckles on the gear. I unfastened the packs and tried to carry one up the scree to the solid part of the trail. The rubble kept sliding beneath me. It was like a nightmare in which I could run, but I could not make forward progress. Yet somehow, with every muscle straining, my belly, legs, arms, hands and even my chin stretched across the sharp, hot rocks, scrabbling my way up the slope, I did make more awkward forward progress than downward backsliding. Struggling, sweating, and grunting with effort, I shot my arm across a bit of a ledge just before the shale could carry me back down.

The pack I brought up had extra rope in it. I tied the rope securely to the tree growing horizontally out of a crack in the rocks above the ledge. It was one of those trees you couldn't imagine surviving where it did. Not only was it alive, but it was also very firmly anchored. I used the rope to lower myself down to Cacho. After three trips and a grimy coating of sweat, all of the gear sat in a pile on firm soil. Cacho, still mired in the rubble but feeling relatively free without the gear, began to struggle. I told him "easy," but not "ho," and watched intently as he freed himself from the tree. He scrambled over some branches to a narrow ledge where he could stand more comfortably, only up to his pasterns in rocky scramble. He started to go farther, and then I said in a low, firm tone, "Ho." Obedient, trusting, he stopped.

I dug into the packs for my hatchet and collapsible saw and, using the rope, ungracefully tumbled to where he stood and began to make a trail for him. The tools were moderately useful, but mostly I used my hands to break branches and scoop gravel, freeing clouds of dust into the air. We tried unsuccessfully once to get back to the main trail. When he began to slide, I took him back to his waiting place and started again. After two hours, another trail and a second try, he lunged past me and up to the little ledge. I hauled myself up the rope after him, then led him past the talus and dropped the rein, letting him stand untethered on solid footing while we both caught our breath.

I wiped a layer of dirt from my face with a bandana, then checked Cacho's legs. He seemed OK, but I couldn't be sure. The rest of the path to the crest was very steep, so it was hard to know whether Cacho's steps were regular or if he was limping. At the top a road ran along the ridge. I waited there for Tony, still worried about Cacho, who rested quietly while I nervously picked at my sunburned nose till it bled. The ridge provided no water, and since Cacho had sweated heavily, he would need more than what remained in my two-quart canteen. I could wait only so long.

After an hour, I realized there was nothing to do but continue in the dark for fifteen bone-weary miles to a ranger station where I knew there would be water. I stumbled alongside Cacho, listening carefully to the rhythm of his footfalls until I could convince myself that he hadn't been injured. Though relieved about Cacho, I was cold and tired, and since Tony hadn't met me as planned, I faced a night without a tent or sleeping bag. I was not in a particularly cheerful mood when, at the shivering stroke of midnight, I arrived at the ranger station. Finding a pay phone, I left a testy, ear-singeing, eyebrow-raising message on Tony's answering machine.

It had the desired effect of bringing him screeching up the mountain at top speed, braking so hard on the gravel in the parking lot that his truck slid several feet before coming

9

to a stop. Huddled under a wet horse blanket, I was cold to the core and in a tempestuous frame of mind.

Tony's step slowed as he approached. He quickly discerned that a pleasant discussion of the day's scenery was unlikely. He made a feeble attempt to explain how he had missed me and ask how I was, but the look in my eyes froze the words on his tongue. He stood for a moment assessing the situation, not daring to look at my steely blues, which were armed with the day's emotions. Then he made the only move that possibly could have broken the deadlock: forgoing conversation, Tony opened his arms and invited a comforting hug. Without thinking, I abandoned my hostility, gratefully slipping my arms around his waist under his soft jacket. He squeezed me gently, reassuringly. Pressed against his flannel shirt, I felt my muscles relax. The consternation I had suffered all evening melted in a warm embrace.

Few people but Tony could have diffused my emotions so effectively. His exceptional ability to handle the situation fit with his extraordinary character. I discovered that he valued literature and history, as evidenced by the musty books and antique saddles in his collection, but since he had few other possessions, I detected little interest in wealth or physical comfort. He had let me spend the previous night on the floor of his unusual, yet somehow appropriate dwelling: a Quonset hut. I had taken a shower in an outdoor shower he had rigged up outside—so I could be fresh and clean for clawing my way out of the gritty gorge.

Tony lay down beside me on the ground, and we pulled our sleeping bags up to our chins, staring through the branches of an oak tree into a dark, starless, foggy sky. He told me interesting and comforting stories until at last I could hold back sleep no more.

* ★ ★

The next two days I would travel the ridgeline road, Camino Cielo. There would be no source of water. It seemed absurd to fret about it, since tiny spheres of water hung so thickly in the cool morning air that they merged together, wetting all exposed surfaces. But because Cacho needed more water each day than I could carry, and he couldn't drink the mist, I worried, but pressed on all the same.

I wore my forest green Gore-tex rain slicker, a black cowboy hat, and black gloves. A lovely dry creek bed vegetated with old oaks and car-sized boulders graced the winding way up to the ridgeline. The rocks looked as though they had Native American grinding holes. A few cars slowed and politely stayed behind me until I waved them past with a casual, commanding flick of my gloved hand. I wished more cars would come by so that I could direct them. (Maybe some police force someday will let me direct traffic when a light is out at an intersection.)

I realized I was in an obnoxiously good mood. I decided there must be nothing like a brush with a near-death experience on a shale slope to perk up one's spirits for a few days.

We climbed out of the creek valley and onto the ridge that runs north to south along much of the southern and central coastline. Sage spiced the air, and annual flowers added bright blue, orange, magenta, and yellow to the soft greens and grays of the perennials. Dramatic, twisted rocks, colored with lichen, punctuated the scrub. Some of the massive boulders had crevices big enough to crawl through. The dirt road disintegrated into a rutted, rocky track, excellent for riding, but virtually impassable to motorized vehicles.

The next day the clouds parted, providing excellent views of the scenic countryside in the valley below the ridge, but

11

allowing the sun to snatch away the dewdrops Cacho had been consuming along with grass. In the afternoon, at last, I stopped Cacho at a water impoundment. It had been about thirty-five hours since he'd last had a drink, but he was in good shape because we had taken a relaxed gait and the weather had cooperated. He took a quick sip, but, to my surprise and relief, was more interested in the grass growing around the artificial pond than in the water.

** **

Thirteen days after bailing out of the safety of my job, my home, and my circle of friends, I fell into the bucolic Santa Ynez Valley and began searching for a place to camp. As Cacho and I approached a tiny ranch house in the midst of sprawling pastures, I heard the sound of a hammer and decided to investigate. I hailed the elderly rancher, who explained that he was building a kennel for a new puppy. He wore a cotton shirt, a straw cowboy hat, and blue jeans held in place by a belt with a silver buckle. I told of my odyssey, showing him Chase's book, and asked if I could camp on his ranch.

"Well, where did you have in mind?" he inquired, his tone playful, his brow furrowed in mock seriousness.

"Over there between those oaks—where all the oats are— looks like a pretty good spot."

"Well," the man said, scratching his chin thoughtfully, "Yep, you could camp there." He paused with a twinkle in his eye, pretending not to be sure what he was going to say next. "Or," he said slowly, "you could stay in this travel trailer. It's got water and electricity hooked up to it. And you could put your horse up in one of my corrals." After almost two weeks on the trail, his offer was as welcome as an open parachute to a skydiver plummeting through the air.

For one evening I entered the kind, warm world of this elderly rancher, Clark, and his wife, Dorothy. They had lived in this valley their whole lives and, now in their seventies or eighties, knew much of its history. They had a tidy little home, spotlessly clean and full of photos of their children and grandchildren. I admired a dust-free blue horse show ribbon, proudly displayed on the eggshell-colored wall. "First place in the Western Reining Competition," Dorothy explained, beaming. "The grandkids ride pretty good, I'll say, but they know better'n tryin' ta outride their grampa."

* * *

Leading my horse, Clark and I strolled down the dirt road that was their driveway. We moved Clark's handsome brown and white paint quarter horses so that Cacho could have his own corral. I led him in through the gate and barely got the halter off before he lowered himself to his knees. He was, I could tell, going to enjoy a good dust bath.

Grunting, he threw his legs in the air and flopped all the way over onto his other side in the dusty corral. He wriggled over again, scrubbing his mane and tail in the dirt and kicking up a cloud of powder. Clark and I leaned on a fence rail watching. The rancher said, "Nuther hundred." Cacho heaved himself over a third time and then stood up and shook, his mane slapping his neck noisily, sending more particles into the air. Clark said, "You got yerself a good three-hundred-dollar horse, there." He explained the custom among horsemen is to ascribe a hundred dollars for each complete roll a horse makes. He expertly grabbed three flakes of good-quality alfalfa hay on the end of a pitchfork and tossed it to my happy, dirty horse. "That way you won't have to feed him in the morning." Clark said, explaining the excess with a wink.

After leaving the sanctuary provided by Dorothy and Clark, Lisa stopped at Mission La Purisma on her way to Pismo Beach. Photo by Lisa Wood

⋆ ⋆ ⋆

The peacefulness of the quiet ranch soothed me, and I readily forgot the trials of traffic. However, this persistent nemesis would not be so easily dismissed. Two days later, when Cacho carried me to Pismo State Park, we were greeted by a churning mass of human activity. Apparently, the rest of the world had also come here for the weekend. Campers checked in, others drove out for dinner, making the park entrance a chaotic din of engines, shouts and laughter. Cacho pulled his ears into a sullen angle and swished his tail in warning, but no one took notice of his language. Under other circumstances I might have enjoyed the crowded celebration and the energy generated by an aggregated mass of beer-drinking partyers, but being responsible for a potentially spooky animal put a damper on my own revelry. A thousand pounds of hoof and muscle can accidentally harm someone quite easily, just by bumping into people or accidentally stepping on them.

As soon as the attendant provided directions, I nudged Cacho on. He picked his way through the hubbub to a secluded mosquito gulch, where we spent a blessedly quiet evening serenaded by a frog chorus.

The next morning began peacefully, the merrymakers hushed under a heavy haze of alcohol, but after about an hour the traffic began to build. Tourists crowded the roads and sidewalks of little beach towns like paparazzi flocking to a celebrity. I threaded my way through the pedestrians on the sidewalk, leading Cacho as if he were a very big dog. People seemed completely unaware of how skittish horses can be. They gave Cacho no space, and one or two actually bumped into him. He fixed his eyes on me and followed loyally. I wondered how we would get through larger urban areas, and decided this was good preparation, but ardently pushed on toward Avila, where I imagined a more subdued ambiance.

The previous winter, I had visited Avila on a cold, windy day. Wet, emerald green palms had rustled violently, and cold rain came in heavy spurts. The manager of a resort built around natural hot springs had agreed to let me camp on the lawn, in front of a complex of buildings constructed around the sulfur hot springs. In December it had been green, spacious, and deserted. However, as I looked down on the spa from the road above on May 30, a serious contrast confronted me.

Memorial Day weekend proved to be slightly overcast but warm, and the palms did not sway, not even a little, in the still air. The biggest change, however, was not the weather, but the volume of clientele. Not a square inch of vacant lawn showed amidst the smoking barbecues, and squealing children darted between the densely packed clusters of picnickers. I wondered vaguely how many youngsters Cacho would maim under his heavy hooves if I tried to squeeze onto the grass. Riding at three miles per hour, you have plenty of time to consider a situation visible in the distance long before you arrive there.

I remembered a sign advertising hour-long horse rides, and so continued to a rental stable down the road. After some negotiations with the proprietors, Kenny and Elizabeth, I arranged to camp there. As soon as I was settled in, customers arrived seeking a ride, initiating a flurry of activity. Kenny loaded their gaunt horses into a large trailer. The customers got in their cars and followed the horse trailer to a destination on the coastal dunes some miles away. I wondered why they didn't take the people on more local trails.

As the commotion subsided, I noticed that two small boys remained. Without a hint of shyness they immediately introduced themselves, explaining that their parents ran the fruit stand across the road. The boys gossiped uninhibitedly about their neighbors, explaining the hardships of the proprietors, whom they adored.

According to their account, the owner of the property had originally allowed the stable to offer rides onsite. However, as he became concerned about liability, he decided to change the terms of the lease, forcing Kenny and Elizabeth to drive the horses to a public area for rides. The fuel costs and lack of convenience associated with this procedure had pushed this already marginal equestrian establishment to its economic limit.

The older boy, Ricky, a thin youth with blond hair, darted across the street to the family business so he could show me his mare. He came back riding her. He rode her everywhere: to the gate and back and hither and yon. Ricky talked and rode, his horse providing the constant movement he desired. He reined the mare harshly to turn her, and I noticed her mouth open as the steel curb hit her soft palate, but she went obediently where he asked. The boy noticed my involuntary wince, and asked advice, eager to learn.

"Try giving a more gentle cue with your legs before you turn her head with the reins," I suggested, "and always look in the direction you're going. She'll follow around better if you just face where you want to go with your head and body."

"Like that?" Ricky asked, anxious to try.

"That's better," I said, not actually noticing a difference.

"Is that your horse?" he asked, pointing to Cacho.

"Yeah, I've got to take him someplace where there's good grass. Kenny and Elizabeth said here's no hay to spare here."

Ricky immediately pulled his mare around and trotted her across the street to a berry stand, returning with a heavy flake of hay on his horse's ample butt. As soon as he arrived, a woman yelled from across the street and the boys disappeared, on their way to dinner.

The day had turned out well in the end. After the turmoil of the beach towns, I had finally found a haven where Cacho and I could camp. With Cacho secure in a stall for the night, I slept soundly, worry-free.

* * *

The next day, the road skirted a soft-looking, green salt marsh. Patches of brazenly bright orange dodder (*Cuscuta*) vines contrasted with the restrained, mature colors of the fleshy pickle weed (*Salicornia bigelovii*). Pure white egrets provided elegant contrast to the darker colors of the soils and vegetation. Their reflections shimmered on the surface of the brackish channels. They posed motionlessly, studying the murky water in search of their fishy prey. The egrets' larger cousins, enormous blue-gray great herons, also visited the marsh. One took flight with a slow, graceful flapping of its long wings, confidently stretching toward the sky. After the initial effort to gain altitude, it folded its long neck into an elegant S-shape.

The last part of the ride to Morro Bay State Park took me along a busy two-lane road. I glanced only briefly at the view, wishing for some trace of a road shoulder, rationalizing that the road had probably been narrowed to minimize impacts to the wetland. I concentrated on the traffic in a sort of forward-thinking prayer that, I hoped, made the cars and me slightly thinner. I thought skinny thoughts, wanting to make more room between the passing vehicles and myself.

At the State Park I found a park attendant, a tall man in his twenties with hazel eyes and a serious expression, wearing a freshly cleaned and pressed khaki park uniform. I asked if there was pizza delivery to the campsites.

In a parody of deep concern he asked gravely, "Do you want cheap or good?"

"The best they deliver." I insisted, then used the phone to order it, and also to summon a farrier.

Cacho needed a new set of shoes. The farrier talked to me at length about my horse's excellent hooves, complimenting me on the practical and docile nature of my mount. Flatter my horse and you flatter me, so I immediately liked him. He held Cacho's hoof firmly on a leather apron between his knees. He worked the oversized clippers and rasp quickly in his long, deft fingers. Cacho had had his feet trimmed many times, and lifted his foot casually for his manicure. The farrier heated the shoe over his portable burner, shaped it, then held it in a clamp and applied the red-hot metal to the bottom of Cacho's hoof. The cartilage singed in a puff of acrid smoke. After he had the hoof and shoe perfectly shaped for each other, he nailed on the shoe with a little tick-tick tapping sound.

The next day, wearing his new shoes, Cacho carried me past impressive Morro Rock. The rock, a small mountain really, loomed out of the flat, light gray, sandy beach. The surf played at the foot of the mammoth brown monolith, painting a white line at the base. Bits of hardy green vegetation clung bravely to its few horizontal surfaces.

* * *

On the nineteenth day of travel I approached a ranch with great confidence, emboldened by my many successes at finding places to camp on ranches. A friendly tack store manager in Morro Bay had directed me to this particular ranch, assuring me the rancher was a good customer who would surely let me camp on his property.

The rancher leaned on his shovel as I approached, and when I asked if I could put up my tent, he said, "Er, no, I don't think I can let you do that." He explained about liability issues, as if I had never before heard of litigation in our society, and said that under no circumstances could he let me spend the night on his property.

"You know, Cacho and I have been doing this for a while.

We started in L.A., and this guy," I patted Cacho's neck, and he seemed to try to look small and innocent, "just doesn't spook or get into trouble, and we would be gone first thing in the morning. Really, we would be no trouble, but it's got to be several miles to the next ranch, and we could never make it there before sunset."

The man said harshly, "Look, lady, I don't care where you stay, but you ain't staying on my property." With that he dusted off his knee, turned his back on me, and stalked off toward a shed.

I rode bitterly back toward the road, going only about half a mile before I had to stop because the pads had slipped back under the saddle. I tugged on the strap holding the saddle on (the strap is called a *latigo*), troubled about where we were going to camp, but Cacho calmly ate green ryegrass. I envied Mr. Chase, the man who inspired my trip. In 1911 he'd had more opportunity to camp on unmarked land and to stay in hotels that catered to equestrians. My barely suppressed insecurities surfaced as I faced a cold night with no campsite, and my eyes probed the countryside as I contemplated trespassing on the man's property with the aid of my wire-cutters.

Fortunately, much sooner than I expected, I found some more congenial property owners and a suitable place to stay. My emotions pitched violently from fear and anger to utter relief, bringing a sudden surge of tears to my eyes when they agreed to let me camp on their property. Seeing it, my hostess asked if I was OK, and my voice trembled a little when I told her that I was just so happy she was allowing me to stay. Moved by my accidental passion, she kindly invited me to do laundry and take a shower. Yippee! For once I was thankful for my own emotional sensitivity.

The next day I remembered the unkind rancher, which

whipped me back into a sour mindset. But I couldn't maintain it. Well rested and riding through sun-drenched scenery, a whistle leaked from between my lips; it was impossible not to feel downright jaunty.

I silenced my tuneless whistling abruptly when I heard a strange, low, grunting sound. Normally, Cacho's ears alerted me to nearby life forms, at least the larger ones, but whatever it was didn't bother Cacho. His ears dangled at a relaxed and inattentive angle. I looked around, and there on the other side of a fence, in the middle of the pasture, stood a large black bull. His small, dark eyes glistened as he snorted, menacingly pawing the ground with a cloven hoof. Poor thing, I thought. Tons of fury poised harmlessly on the far side of the barbed wire. If I hadn't bothered looking around I wouldn't even have seen him. Cacho seemed to ridicule the animal by completely ignoring him. Chuckling, I smoothed the fur at the base of Cacho's neck, and he carried me forward.

* * *

There were trees but no ranches as we entered a strange, poison forest. The rutted dirt road ran near Cypress Mountain, elevation 2,933 feet. The ruins of abandoned mines, surrounded by ugly mountains of tailings, with strange, toxic-looking, brightly-colored creeks near them, told the reason why there were no people. Mercury occurs naturally in this area, and the mines exposed large quantities of it, poisoning the water not only with mercury, but also cyanide, used in the bleaching process. Rusty-red—presumably from iron—and turquoise-colored leachate sat in ditches. Rivulets of iridescent ooze painted a psychedelic landscape, oddly attractive in a frightening, surreal way.

After several hours, having seen not one vehicle, I found

a grassy area for a comfort stop. Disregarding usual practice, I didn't bother finding a bush or a tree to ensure privacy. How much more secluded could I get than being several miles into a tainted forest?

As soon as I was indisposed, I heard an engine. I looked around desperately as I realized a truck was coming up the road and would soon round the corner. All I had time to do was grab some gear and put it across my lap.

The driver, seeing a rider in this remote area, stopped to chat. He turned off the engine and leaned out the window to ask me how far I had come and all the standard sociable questions. He seemed completely unaware of my reason for sitting on the roadside with gear across my lap.

In utter embarrassment, the circumstances forced me to admit, "Actually, I could use a moment of privacy. Would you mind driving around the corner and coming back in a few minutes?"

Comprehension spread slowly across his face, "Oh, sure," he said, "I'll just drive around the corner and be right back." I would rather have been buried in some mercury-contaminated soil than face this man again, but I stayed put until he returned, and then feigned some excuse for cutting the conversation short.

Distancing myself from the episode, I rode through the dappled sunlight in a pine-forested area. An embankment on the side of the road led to a clear, fresh stream—no signs of noxious chemicals. A few yards ahead of me I spotted a male fox down in the drainage. He saw me and, with a glance over his shoulder, scampered up the embankment directly in front of me and began trotting down the road, drawing me into a little Nature Drama.

The fox kept a safe distance between us, but repeatedly looked back as if to make sure I was following. I knew the ruse, perhaps because I had seen it on NBC's *Wonderful World of Disney*. He was, I assumed, the decoy, so I looked down the embankment, away from which he was leading me. Sure enough, Mama Fox popped her head out of the den, and watched as Papa Fox escorted Cacho and me safely past. Once we were well past the lair, Papa Fox scurried down the embankment and disappeared into the brush. I could almost hear the folksy narration: "The rider safely on her way, Father Fox returned to his job of catching mice for the pups."

* * *

That night I camped on the bank of a small farm pond. The still water provided a peaceful, shimming reflection of a weeping willow. I had just finished cooking my dehydrated dinner when Cacho's head shot up in alarm. A large animal, no, make that *animals,* were making their way through the brush and under the willow on the other side of the pond. Sonorous snorting accompanied a loud snapping of branches. Soon a family of feral pigs, complete with ferocious-looking tusks, made their way to the water, arguing loudly with one another as they came.

I told Cacho, who shifted his weight and flared his nostrils nervously, "It's all right; you can relax, buddy." I had no idea whether the situation was truly dangerous, but I insisted that it wasn't. Skeptical, Cacho and I both kept a wary eye out as the pigs snuffled and snorted their way partway around the pond and then returned peaceably the way they had come.

* * *

The trip so far had posed many challenges, from negotiating drive-throughs on horseback, to life-threatening slides into a deep gorge, to an unkind rejection at a campsite, and even a brush with big, bad, wild animals—well, OK, just feral pigs. They are pretty scary, tusk-bearing creatures to look at, trust me. The next challenge, on day twenty-two, was crossing Nacimiento dam, although, it ended up being no trouble for Cacho. I had bought him only two or three months before beginning the trip, so I was just getting to know him as we traveled. His wisdom and dependability surpassed that of the literally hundreds of horses I had known before. I felt incredibly lucky to have hooked up with him.

The dam was a massive concrete structure holding back thousands of tons of water, and I had thought it might frighten Cacho, but he walked across unperturbed. I imagined how I looked from above the dam, perhaps from a helicopter hovering over the scene. Wearing my forest green rain slicker, riding my horse on an antique saddle, I was a tiny speck from an earlier era as I rode across the imposing engineering marvel.

A few miles past the dam the pressure in my bladder demanded attention, but the thin shrubbery held no promise of privacy. I determined not to be caught with my pants down again, but a stinking corpse defiled the first secluded place! All the same, I could wait no longer and simply endured the odor. The carcass belonged to the wild animal responsible for more human deaths than any other in the state, not a mountain lion or other carnivorous beast, but the large animal most likely to jump in front of a passing car: the mule deer. I decided it was this one's smell that was lethal.

Hastily continuing on, I marveled at the majestic oaks adorning the hills. Colonies of magpies filled the branches and made crazy circles over the golden oat meadows. Deep, iridescent black, with bold white markings and bright yellow beaks, the birds stood out both visually and acoustically. They scolded and chattered loudly, "chaw-chaw-chaw!" as Cacho and I passed by.

Listening to their laughter, I thought back over the last few days. I heard the laughter of the girls from the Taco Bell, and remembered the amusement of the truck driver who had seen me indisposed on the side of the road. Since enlightenment is supposed to be the reward for suffering a solitary pilgrimage, I was eager to find my epiphany. I tried out this one: Don't take yourself too seriously, like the self-important bull pawing on the far side of the fence. Ugh, pretty lame. I caressed Cacho's mane and told him I was going to have to keep going till I came up with something better than that.

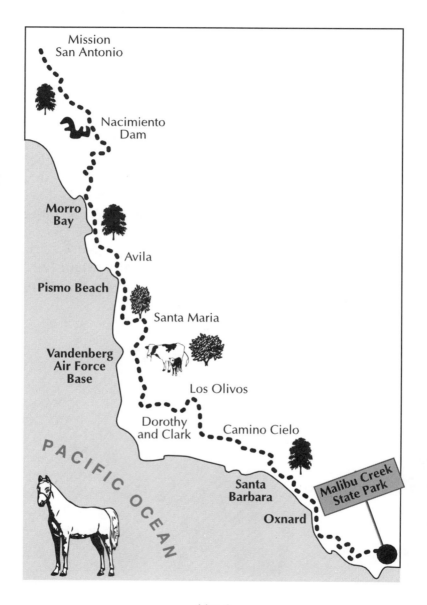

Map 2

2
Reaching for a Friend

It hadn't been easy to disentangle myself from obligations to dash up the coast on a horse. Additionally, leaving friends and family with no forwarding address proved emotionally difficult. I needed my friends, and my friends needed me, as I discovered when, the week before I left, Jory, the fifteen-month-old son of close friends, was diagnosed with terminal brain cancer. I wanted to "be there" for my friends, Susan and Derek, but they urged me not to abandon my plans. With a sense of foreboding I plunged on, but I carried their burden with me in my heart, and called often to find out how the illness progressed. As Thornton Wilder said, when one is at home, one dreams of adventure, when one is on an adventure, one dreams of home. Days of riding accompanied exclusively by a horse provided opportunities for me to consider my friends' grief. Solitude is valuable in that way, but in this case it did not bring resolution or emotional closure.

In a contemplative mood, I passed the guard station at Hunter Liggett during a soaking thunderstorm. An elderly man, short, with slightly stooped shoulders and gray hair, walked methodically in the direction of the historic Catholic California mission located there. Cacho moved slowly for a horse, but we were able to catch up with this deliberate man. I dismounted and fell into step with him, and we strolled along companionably for a short distance without speaking. I cautiously broke the silence to ask if he was a father at the mission.

"Yes," he said thoughtfully, not ending the answer with "my child," but leaving the words somehow hanging in the air. Benevolence shone from his eyes like sunbeams.

"Well, I was wondering if I—I mean, we—might be able to spend the night."

He looked at me with a loving, appraising gaze. Cacho and I had traveled approximately twenty-two miles that rainy day, and we both looked tired and soggy. He said, "You are traveling. That is one of the mission's functions: to provide refuge, to provide sanctuary."

I nodded, my face showing my relief.

The priest looked at me and smiled, then turned his eyes toward the mission and said solemnly, "A guest has arrived, Jesus is here."

Once on the grounds, the priest showed me the archeological sites: the gristmill, which had used waterpower to grind wheat, the Indian cemetery where the priests and the early converts were buried. He displayed no hint of awareness of the criticism of the California mission's treatment of Native Americans. Modestly, he told me that the church's work with the local tribes "is quite small, but it still continues."

The mission was a large adobe structure encircling a weedy courtyard. The residents kept to a strict schedule: dinner at 7 P.M., silence at 9 P.M., breakfast at 7 A.M., and mass at 8:30 A.M. A brother directed me to a clean, Spartan room, and I had just enough time for a quick shower before dinner. The fathers and brothers shared roast beef, salad, potatoes, and other simple, delicious morsels with me. A brother asked me, "How have you been treated?"

Lisa and Cacho loaded up and ready to travel.
Notice Cacho's excellent muscle definition. Cacho
had spent the night tied to the rail.
Lisa spent the night on the porch.
— Photo taken by the owner of the Palaminos.

"Amazingly well. Total strangers have not only allowed me to camp on their property, but have also invited me in for dinner." And almost every day that had been so. "I am looking for differences between 1911 and now, and I thought hospitality would be one of them. I didn't expect people to be so open and giving, but I've really seen the good side of people. Everyone has been very generous."

"No one turned you away?" The way he asked this question, thoughts of Mary and Joseph in Bethlehem crossed my mind.

"Well, I wouldn't say everyone has been delighted." I

told my dinner companions about the rancher who had refused to let me camp on his property. "But really, for the most part, I've seen the best side of people. It's the sort of thing that restores your faith in the goodness of people."

The next morning during mass I joined the brown-robed fathers and brothers on folding chairs in the front of the sanctuary. The images of Bible figures and saints looked down as I thought of my friends, Susan and Derek, and their dying baby Jory, who was undergoing futile chemotherapy. My heart went out to them. My head bowed, tears streamed down my face as if a dam had broken, releasing my grief. Even with my eyes closed I could feel the concern of the holy men, and I knew they were supporting my prayer with theirs. When the prayer concluded, the men did not comment on my obvious distress, but they gave me compassionate looks as we left the sanctuary.

One of the priests escorted me as I prepared to depart. "A visitor came, Jesus was here," he said, using the past tense in his benediction. He raised his hand and blessed my horse and prayed for our safety, and then he handed me a St. Antonio medal. I felt blessed, and more at peace with the pending tragedy of the death of a child. Somehow my communion at the mission brought an emotional fulfillment that my solitary grieving had not.

* * *

I climbed into the saddle and rode into the purple mountains that rose, rinsed by the recent rain, into the clean, blue sky. The dirt road led through a fragrant grove of pines. Above the hushed whisper of the breeze in the needles, I heard the sound of an approaching engine. Out of the pale green government truck stepped a ranger with whom I had spoken on the phone. He produced a map and spread it on the hood of his truck in the cool shade. Intent on socializing, Cacho stuck his big head between us, wiping a little smudge of dirt on the map and then affectionately nuzzling the ranger's uniform. The ranger had a horse of his own and didn't mind; he scratched the itchy spot on Cacho's forehead.

I shoved Cacho away by pushing my fist into his chest. With a bemused voice that pretended to be cross, I told him, "Go take a nap or something."

Napping was one of his favorite activities ("napping activity"—is that an oxymoron?), second only to eating, so he obligingly moved a few steps away, carefully holding his reins to the side to avoid stepping on them, and promptly closed his eyes.

"Well-trained horse." The ranger remarked. I smiled, knowing that Cacho always liked to nap in the afternoons.

* * *

Four days later Cacho bore me onto a beach in Carmel. On the edge of town we found a small beach where two games of two-man volleyball were in progress. The players, tanned, muscular young men, wore colorful shorts and name-brand sunglasses. Sweat gleamed off their skin as they jumped in the air to hit the white leather ball over the net.

A short distance away, a group of people in formal attire congregated on neat rows of folding chairs, struggling to keep sand out of their shoes. They took their seats and fell silent just as I rode by. Stately music began playing from a set of portable speakers as the bride, in a long white gown, carefully made her way down the red carpet laid over the sand, toward a white arching trellis.

The juxtaposition struck me as extreme: me in dirty, earth-toned cowboy clothes, the volleyball players, nude except for sweat-stained, vibrantly colored shorts, and the bride and groom in stately black-and-white.

I turned my attention back to the volleyball players. Except for their fearsome spiking, I thought I could do almost as well, and suddenly missed my regular games in San Diego. I tied Cacho to a tree and took off my hat, gloves, shoes and socks. Still wearing my jeans and long-sleeved shirt, I approached four bare-chested players and asked if I could play a game. They didn't seem perturbed by my abrupt inquiry, and said they could think of no reason why I could not. With no questions, a man graciously dropped off the court, and I took his place.

The men played better and more aggressively than I did; however, the scores were fairly close. I didn't want to take up too much of their court time, so after only two games I thanked them and excused myself.

I guided Cacho toward the exclusive, private community of Pebble Beach. At the guardhouse I explained that I had arranged several months ago for my horse to stay at the equestrian center. The helpful guard asked my indulgence while he called to confirm my arrangements.

"I have a young lady here who needs to get her horse to the equestrian center," the guard explained. "Is it all right to let her through?"

After a pause he put his hand over the receiver and said to me, "She says people aren't allowed to take their horses in."

Unfortunately, the charming Australian woman with whom I had made arrangements was out on a ride. The less-than-charming woman on the phone was challenged when it came to such normally common attributes as logic and compassion. After a frustratingly Orwellian conversation, she finally agreed to let me in, provided I would allow a security guard to escort me. Though an escort seemed unnecessary, I had no objection.

The security guard fought boredom more often than crime, so he accepted the time-consuming task good-naturedly. Slowly, we paraded through the shady streets, the white pickup in front, with its yellow warning lights flashing. From my elevated vantage point on Cacho's back, I could see over stone walls and into the grounds of the mansions owned by the rich and famous. Lush gardens, lovingly tended by unhurried servants, lost their privacy under my prying eyes.

The elegant community took little notice of my formal entrance, or of my quiet departure the next day. Cacho's hooves dug deeply into the white sand, under a Monterey pine forest. The track led me out of the woods and alongside the famed scenic golf course. The low sound of the surf surging in great waves against the shore gave a throbbing, back-beat to the view. Healthy, fat, remarkably tame deer nibbled on the carefully tended golf course. The soft brown animals stood passively as if mechanical, flicking their big ears and lifting their wet nostrils as golfers played through and I rode by.

The surf crashed against the rock formations of the coastline in brilliant, sunlit white sprays, and the wind added its vigorous, salty bite to the air. Cacho and I threaded our way along the golf course, I with my eyes to the left, watching the sea; Cacho keeping an eye on the deer and the golfers.

From there, I went as quickly as possible through the crowded boardwalk on Cannery Row, and on to the Fort Ord military base. Cacho and I had traveled fourteen miles, not an impressive total, but with our formidable antagonist, in the form of crowds and traffic, for us to battle all day, we were both spent. When we came dragging up to the guard station, the men clearly were not expecting me. Trying to look serious—not bemused, as I suspected they were—they listened to my explanation. One of them stepped into the booth to make a call to confirm my story. He hung up the phone and whispered to his partner, then together they stepped out of the booth and saluted me! One of them barked deferentially, "Yes, ma'am. Permission granted to camp where you like. The colonel knows all about you and says we are to extend every courtesy." I was glad I had done my homework in preparing for this journey. It would not have been a good day to be turned away.

These soldiers followed the line of inquiry that others had. The military personnel I encountered were always impressed with my "courage." Yeah, right! I am so bold I wince at the thought of having my teeth cleaned. What made them think I was brave? These strong, muscular men—who could bench-press my horse and face enemy fire—noted that I had no human companions, no unit of buddies supporting me. It was being alone that they considered valorous, not facing mountain lions.

But I was not completely alone. Besides my close companionship with Cacho, I reached for and found friends along the way. I quickly formed tendrils of connection with strangers. There was a difference, though, between the companionship of people I met as a sojourner and the company of my long-term friends. The former were like a parachute, supporting me as I fell, but my friends were the ground beneath my feet, stopping my fall altogether. As long as I traveled, the military personnel knew that there was some social aspect, some support, that I was missing.

My father drove to Monterey and brought me a box of letters and advertisements. Upon getting a month of accumulated mail, I began to understand more clearly my own need for enduring friendship. I discarded the junk mail and opened the letters, discovering that my longtime friend, Michael, had died. Although I knew he was HIV-positive, I didn't know he had developed AIDS, so the news came as a shock.

I felt very alone. Time on the trail to meditate to the four-footed rhythm of Cacho's stride could not replace the fellowship of mutual friends. Mike's death, like Jory's illness, was a burden I could not explain to the kind strangers who opened their lives to me for only a day or less. It was a sadness that needed to be shared with old friends—or understanding priests. I needed a support group or, failing that, another visit to a mission. It wasn't likely I would get either in the near future.

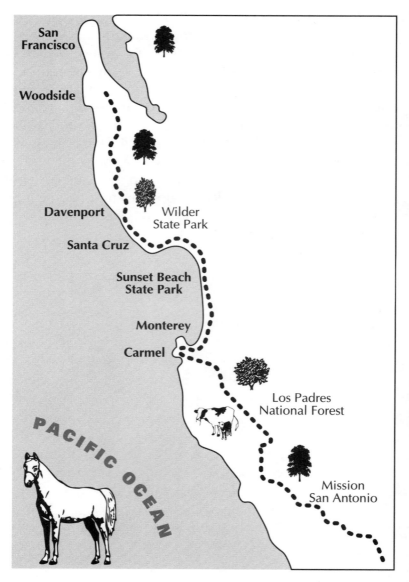

Map 3

3

Reaching the Point of Pain

From Fort Ord I headed to the home of Nancy, a friend of a person I had met on the trail a week earlier. She had sounded happy to have an equestrian visitor, since there were few other horses in this crop-growing area. The plan was for me to stay two days on her property and go on a ride with her. I arrived at her house feeling confident and safe. I shouldn't have, though my accommodations were secure, and rural areas banished my archenemy, traffic. Even so, like a snake coiled and waiting, disaster was poised to strike.

As soon as we left her yard Nancy had to fight to keep her thoroughbred at a walk, finally allowing her to take an irregular, but fast, trot. The mare spooked and snorted as she moved, clearly fearing that horse-eating predators lurked in the fields and, as we neared the coast, hid behind each sand dune. I rode Cacho bareback, wanting to avoid any unnecessary wear from the saddle, and as he trotted and cantered to keep up, I struggled to stay on him. In contrast to his usual, energy-saving deportment, he wiggled and kicked up his heels, agreeing with the thoroughbred that horse devils inhabited the area. He fought against the gentle *hackamore* (a bitless bridle, a bosal), shaking his head.

Nancy had had enough excitement, so we returned to the house, and the thoroughbred strode quickly back to the yard, seemingly satisfied to be done with the entire experience. It had been a brief ride, maybe forty-five minutes altogether. "I think I'll take Cacho out and see what his problem is," I said as she dismounted and dragged the English-style saddle off her horse.

I took Cacho out to a place where a long, straight dirt road ran alongside a field of lettuce. I let out his reins and, still excited, he pushed from a trot to a canter, and then full out, as fast as his little legs would carry him. The thoroughbred could easily have surpassed him with her long strides, but I enjoyed even the moderate speed Cacho could muster.

Not that I rode with carefree abandon; I concentrated on Cacho. He still seemed edgy, and even with a loose rein he shook his head. He raced down the dirt road and then, without warning, he tucked his head and gave a little buck with his hind feet.

Riding with my legs loose as I did, his movement unseated me. I hurtled through the air over his right shoulder. Having gone off many horses, my impending appointment with the hard ground did not concern me. I had chosen this spot to work with Cacho because there were no dangerous obstacles—oh, except the ground itself. Cacho's motion flung me head over heels. I landed on my right shoulder and then rolled with a crash down onto my back.

Breath took a frighteningly long moment to return to my lungs. Once air filled me, I concentrated on my breathing, clenching my teeth and trying not to faint. On a scale of 1 to 10 the pain had a triple-digit exponent. Darkness pressed in on my peripheral vision. I focused on seeing the soft blue sky above me. "Don't pass out," I repeated to myself over and over, pushing back the edges of the blackness with my willpower.

My behavior puzzled Cacho. He had been running and kicking up his heels, and the next thing he knew, there I was on the ground. He came cautiously back to where I lay in the dirt road. He stood there for a while, sniffing my head, as if waiting for me to get up. After a few minutes he took a step away from me. I knew that he would wander off in search of something to eat.

With my left hand I grabbed the rope rein, which dragged on the ground, and jerked it, saying in a low, husky voice, "Ho!" Surprised by my tone, Cacho stopped suddenly, and stood patiently while I closed my eyes to clear them of the stars caused by the effort of grabbing the rope. Apparently my head was not going to clear. I had to stand up despite the dizziness and make my way back to Nancy's before my brain became even more muddled.

I dragged myself to my feet and somehow stumbled to the house. With my left hand I opened the gate to the back yard and led Cacho through. I closed the gate, dropped Cacho's sheepskin-padded bosal on the ground in the weeds in the front yard, stumbled through the open living-room door, and lay down gingerly on the sofa. I congratulated myself. "Now you can pass out." I *wanted* to become unconscious, but I didn't. I just wallowed silently in a purgatory of pain.

* * *

Though the pain subsided, I was too shaken up to travel. Nancy kindly let me stay an extra night and call my parents with the news. At their insistence I went to a medical facility and had my shoulder X-rayed to confirm the break: two cracks in my scapula. By the second day, to the horror of my more sensible parents, I felt ready to continue on my way, albeit with some concerns about how to load the gear one-handed.

To start out, Nancy hoisted the gear on for me and tied it down securely. She smiled and wished me well, and agreed to meet me a few miles up the coast to help with the next day's gear loading.

There would be some challenges before I would see her again. Unfortunately, the only way to go included a quarter-mile along the freeway. I read the sign prohibiting bicycles and pedestrians, making a mental note that it did not specifically prohibit equestrians. I escaped down an embankment at the first opportunity. Vegetation made difficult going on the steep slope, but it seemed to lead to a road that went under the freeway. Cacho skied down the embankment with his front feet extended, not slowed by the snapping of shrubs and reeds, leaving bent stems in his wake. Toward the bottom the terrain became more level, and Cacho could have walked more naturally, but the muddy ground sucked him down to his cannon bones.

As he plunged through the bramble, I surveyed our route. A fence along the road seemed the final, impenetrable obstacle. Taught wire had been securely stapled to the sturdy posts. I saw no place where I could unwire portions of it, and I was unwilling to damage the fence by snipping it with my wire-cutters. I scanned beneath the underpass to the other side, and spied a place where I might get through the fence. To get there we would have to go under the bridge on a manufactured embankment so steep I wondered if Cacho could make it. To make matters worse, a lush carpet of poison oak covered this shady slope.

I dismounted and led Cacho onto the incline. The soil crumbled underfoot, threatening to send us sliding down the poison slope. I held his lead rope in my left hand, my right hand tucked protectively against my torso. I slipped and caught myself by jerking Cacho's head with the lead rope. He accepted the indignity with uncharacteristic good humor, almost as if teasing me for my clumsiness. There goes my nomination for Miss Graceful of 1993.

When we got to the other side, the struggle wasn't over. We still had to get to the other side of the fence. Cacho nibbled on oats while I started working. With only a few scratches on my arms, I got the top two strands of wire unwrapped from the metal post. As the tension released, the uprights began to pull apart. Undoing the two lower strands of barbed wire would destroy the fence, or at least make rewiring it more difficult—impossible for someone with only one strong arm.

"Cacho, buddy, you're going to have to step over this barbed wire. Just keep calm and we'll be all right." Knowing horses could sever tendons on wires, I put my faith in his amazing ability to avoid harm. I let him see the situation for himself. Then, slowly, listening to my coaching as he went, he stepped across, one hoof at a time. He grazed, indifferent to my praise while I wired the fence back together.

The difficult part had been accomplished, but I still felt tense. The muscles in my body contracted, protecting my damaged right shoulder. Cacho sensed my tension through the saddle and responded with nervousness. A tractor came slowly lumbering out from a field of artichokes, and Cacho spooked. His sudden movement jarred my bones, sending a spasm of pain searing through my body.

"Cacho, mellow out, Buddy. It's just a tractor." To get him to understand, I had to speak his language, a nonverbal one. I concentrated on relaxing; Cacho seemed to get a grip on himself and responded by carrying his head lower.

Gradually he quit eyeing the countryside in search of bo-
geymen. The ride became more predictable and less painful.
We turned west, down a pretty, tree-lined road to the park
just as the sun set. Nancy joined us. She camped with us
and helped me get started again the next day.

* * *

Riding toward Santa Cruz, I learned more about the limitations imposed by a broken shoulder. When the paved road
surface sloped downward, Cacho's steel shoes slipped, and
he caught himself with a jerk, causing the too-familiar spasm
of pain. After a couple of these trip-ups I decided to dis-
mount and lead Cacho when there was any risk of slipping.

At a cylindrical concrete planter full of yellow flowers,
Cacho surprised me by suddenly yanking out a mouthful.
He found them to his liking, and slowed at this snack bar.
Suppressing a chuckle, I pulled his head away using my
good arm.

In Santa Cruz, we stopped for a break in a park. I led Cacho
up the concrete steps of a fountain situated in a gazebo. Water shot up in the middle of the circular cement ornament.
Any other horse might have been suspicious, frightened by
the noise and movement, but Cacho climbed the stairs and
stepped right up as if all horses drank from park fountains.

We spent two days in Santa Cruz. Cacho and I stayed
the first night in a suburban backyard belonging to a friend
of Nancy's. The next night we arrived at Wilder State Park.
Beside an ancient barn, I found a grassy paddock for Cacho.
A few pampered head of livestock (sheep, a cow and horses)
roamed the ample pastures. A milking shed had hundreds
of wooden slats for cows to stick their heads through while
being milked, but there was only one cow.

The oversized barn doors invited me to enter the cavern-ous building. Inside, the immense timbers overhead attracted my attention, reminding me of soaring cathedral ceilings. Hundreds of swallows nested in the nooks and crannies of the beams, animating the rafters with motion and sound. Dozens of stalls lined the walls in the back of the barn, and in the front, small rooms had places for hanging gear. Except for the birds, nothing stirred. Cobwebs and dust coated every surface.

I made myself comfortable on some hay, propping my little fluorescent lantern so that I could read by its pale light without holding it. The barn was wired for electric lights, but I didn't want to have to get up to turn them off. Stretched out on a bale of straw, I made sure to keep my sleeping bag away from the numerous little mounds of swallow dung. The dim light made the dirty, antique cobwebs in the high corners of the vast room seem romantic. Sleeping on hay added a sensual implication that filled my mind with wonderful dreams.

* * *

The next day I found someone to help me load the gear, then marched out with a brave heart onto the shoulder of Highway 1. A California Highway Patrol car passed us, then pulled off the road at a wide spot a few hundred yards ahead of us. The officer got out of the car and stood squarely fac-ing us as we approached.

"What are you doing along the highway?" he asked, no warmth or interest in his tone, no expression visible behind his reflective sunglasses.

I gave him an abbreviated version of my story, carefully omitting any reference to my broken bone. I did not want to seem vulnerable; I didn't want to give him a reason to tell me I couldn't be there. As he listened, I noticed a softening around the edges of his mouth below his thick, dark mustache. In an officially paternalistic tone, he said, "OK, then, but stay as far to the right as possible. A driver called in and said you were a hazard on the road."

After about twelve miles, Cacho and I reached Davenport, where I stayed with another friend of Nancy's, a wind-surfer sail maker named Joe. No furniture cluttered his living room, only some long bolts of fabric and a sewing machine on the bare plywood floor for making sails. In the practical, uncluttered kitchen, a few basic appliances sat on the counters, but no packaged foods or piles of beer bottles, only fresh produce and bundles of dried herbs. He had dark green eyes, long lashes, and thick, black hair that curled almost to his shoulders. I found him handsome, and was pleased when he asked, "Hey, Lisa, some friends and I are going to see *Jurassic Park* in town tonight; you want to come?"

Despite feeling guilty and uneasy about leaving Cacho tied to a tree, I accepted. The six of us stood in the long, jostling line for the newly released movie; afterward we strolled to a restaurant and had omelets, salads and beer. The conversation centered on liberal politics and gentle jokes. As I laughed and talked, a constant worry about Cacho pricked my consciousness. I hadn't been separated for him for this long in thirty-nine days. Leaving him bothered me— probably as much as a new mother leaving her child with a babysitter for the first time. I reminded myself that cowboys left their horses hitched to a rail for hours at a time, but it didn't relieve my anxiety. When Joe brought me home, I sighed with relief to find Cacho sleeping peacefully under the tree.

* ⋆ *

The next day, in Woodside, an upscale community in the San Francisco Bay Area, a local woman named Linda accompanied me, riding her stout chestnut quarter horse. She had keys to a gate that opened onto trails on private property. On the other side of the gate, I felt as though I had fallen down a rabbit hole and ended up in Wonderland. Gone was the traffic; gone were difficult terrain and poison-oak-infested streams. A mulched, meandering passage led through a vast expanse of deep emerald green lawn draped over acres of hills. The kind of mower you ride had left its stripes on the weed-free hybrid rye lawn. Stone mansions with leaded glass windows held court amid formal manicured gardens and grand deciduous trees. Sculptures were provided for the viewing pleasure of equestrian visitors. The artwork was of the "modern" variety—unrealistic hunks of metal and brightly painted wood. Not a sophisticated art critic, Cacho found one or two of the pieces spooky. Even I found a few of them startling. Linda took me on the X-rated loop, where towering abstract sculptures did obscene things to each other. Their body parts were sized out of proportion, making the actions they suggested seem painful in the extreme.

Two other well-heeled local horse enthusiasts enjoyed the trail. The white-faced women riders with perfect make-up, hair, and posture wore beige-colored, tight-fitting riding pants with leather knees and crotches, and spotless white, starched blouses. Their stately, well-fed pedigreed horses with freshly combed, licorice-black manes carried shiny, oiled English saddles on their aristocratic backs. The women smiled brilliantly down, swiveling their eyeballs under their lids without lowering their noses, keeping their chins up as if

45

being judged for their poise. They remarked, "Lovely day, isn't it?"

"Exquisite," Linda said with a tinge of affected British, shooting me a quick knowing glance. I thought it would take Cacho about five seconds to mess these women up, rubbing his grass-smudged nose against their starched white blouses. Cacho always got itchy around white. These pedigreed horses' "white attraction" must not be as strong as Cacho's, I thought to myself. Either that or someone else had groomed and saddled the horses for the women.

We padded quietly along a shady trail littered with fragrant pine needles. A hawk on a madrone branch and a fox trotting along the creek took no notice. We emerged from the forest on a spectacularly sunny ridge. We stopped our horses facing northwest, with a view to the right of Palo Alto and beyond to the San Francisco Bay. A froth of thick, melted marshmallow fog had already swallowed San Francisco, and inched majestically, mystically (and mist-ically) along the ground toward us.

I had hoped to take a ferry across the bay, but Linda provided a more practical solution. We loaded Cacho in her trailer, and she dropped me at my parents' house, in Marin County. Cacho stayed at a stable within walking distance. While my parents vacationed in Hawaii, I had their big home, nestled in an oak grove, to myself. I washed my gear, including the saddle pad, halter, and ropes, in Mom's washer. I found the key to my VW Golf, and drove it, shifting with my left hand, to the grocery store. Fruits and vegetables, pickles, sparkling water, and all the things I had been missing as I munched granola bars and jerky at my campsites filled my shopping cart. A red-tailed hawk soared overhead, screeching as if in welcome to the county. All indicators suggested that Cacho and I would both get a nice break in our travels. The omens, as it turned out, were meant only for me, not for Cacho.

Cacho shared a large dirt pasture with five other horses. The proprietor had told me that Appaloosas are troublemakers, and they can be mean. She said she would have to watch my horse. I thought defensive thoughts about my irascible-but-big-hearted spotted animal. The day after I moved Cacho in, a big white horse from Oklahoma arrived. Impatient to establish his dominance, he chased the other horses, which dodged his hooves and teeth. When I came to check on him, I found Cacho standing alone in a corner. He'd already had his encounter with the horse from Oklahoma, and had a nasty bite, right in the middle of his back.

I arranged a separate enclosure with the bigoted proprietor (who blamed Cacho and not the offending horse!) and let him heal for a few days. I used the time to check on my own injury by visiting an orthopedic specialist.

"Hmm. How long ago did this happen?" she asked.

"A little over two weeks ago, I think. Yeah, fifteen days."

"Can you do this?" The doctor held her arm out, demonstrating the motion.

"I don't know," I said, cradling my arm against my body, remembering pain. Cautiously I extended my arm, experiencing some discomfort.

"Can you go like this?" She held her arm out another way. I could. "That is really excellent. Normally I show my patients some exercises, physical therapy, to do to regain their range of motion. You must have a good routine. Whatever you've been doing, keep doing it. You're healing beautifully." And with that she whisked out of the room.

I smiled to myself, thinking she clearly had no idea "whatever you've been doing" entailed, but hey, doctor's orders. Time to make plans to hit the road and resume my "physical therapy."

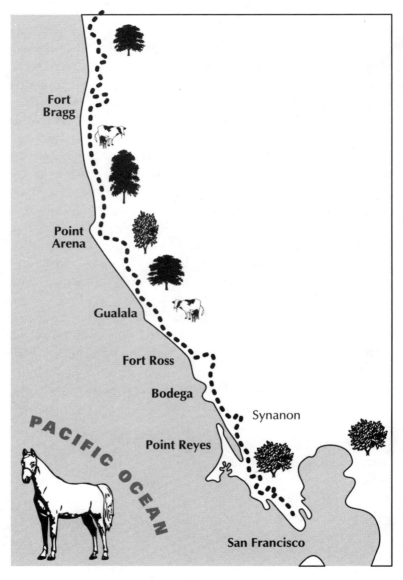

Map 4

4

Reaching a Dilemma

J. Smeaton Chase, who inspired my travels, had worn out his horse, Chino, with saddle sores, so he sold his companion of several years, buying a new horse with whom to finish his travels. He could do this because the goal of his adventure was to explore the coast of California *by* horse. Slowly, I discovered that the goal of my adventure differed slightly. My goal was to visit the coast *with* my horse. The meaning of this distinction began to unfold over the next few days.

I continued unhindered by my broken shoulder because a surveyor I had met in Santa Monica had offered to help if I needed anything. Being ludicrously independent-minded I hated to admit it, but I did need assistance. True to his word, he dropped everything to respond to my SOS. he drove up to help me for a couple of days while my arm, speaking to me in the language of pain, refused to reach high enough to tie on the bedroll.

Although I was thirty-something and single, the blond, muscular surveyor, Luke, was a gentleman. For my part, I quickly became preoccupied with my own difficulties, and wouldn't have recognized a romantic opportunity if it kissed me on the lips. So don't imagine that we tramped off together into a magically beautiful forest for hormonal fulfillment; that's not what happened.

Luke helping Lisa put gear on Cacho

Luke and Lisa headed north through Point Reyes

We began at the Palomarin trailhead in the southern part of Point Reyes. Viewed from above, Point Reyes is a peninsula with a thick neck pinched by two bays. Tomales Bay reaches down like a long finger into Point Reyes from the north, and Drake's Estero reaches up like a hand from the southwest. Inverness Ridge separates the two bays into distinct watersheds. Tomales Bay follows the San Andreas Fault for several miles. Where the fault isn't submerged, dramatic displaced fence lines attest to strong and rapid geologic forces.

Luke led the way through Point Reyes, always selecting the smaller, rougher-looking trails, commenting that
we should take "the road less traveled." Cacho thought
the road might be less traveled for a reason, but I insisted
we defer to the human. Luke stopped to rest at rocky out-
crops providing spectacular views, but walked briskly past
shady areas rich in grass. Cacho did not think much of his
herd-leadership skills.

Low, scrubby shrubs clung to the south-facing slopes as
if afraid to stand any taller, while on north-facing slopes the
bold vegetation grew tall and thick. In riparian corridors,
exulting cottonwoods lifted their branches to the skies. Under their shaking leaves we found respite from the sun and
the prevailing western breeze. In inland areas and on some
northern and eastern slopes, pine trees stood erect, pointing to the clear sky.

This Fourth of July weekend attracted a handful of hikers
wearing expensive synthetic gear. Their high-tech clothing
contrasted sharply with Luke's casual, inexpensive cotton
shorts. Luke led us to a beach where we dabbled our feet/
hooves in the surf. When a family of five followed, riding
their horses and ponies onto the sand, bedlam ensued. The
kids' well-groomed ponies insisted on destroying their freshly
curried appearance by rolling in the sand. Horses thrashed,
their legs pawing the air as they tried to roll over their saddles;
riders shouted and yanked ineffectively on slim leather reins,
while the steady sea heedlessly, rhythmically spilled onto
the beach as if ignoring the pandemonium. Luke glanced
my way, smiled and snorted. I turned to Cacho and said,
"Don't even think about it." He gave me an innocent look.

Luke rejected campgrounds lacking in atmosphere and
privacy and, not tired despite having hiked more than ten

miles with a full pack, led on along a shady trail. Quail startled out of the shrubbery, their little black crest feathers curled forward over their heads as if they wore dress uniforms. Finally, behind Glen Camp, Luke found a grove of redwoods that he thought would make an acceptable campsite.

I took the gear off Cacho, and hung my hat and his bridle on the nubs left where branches had fallen from a tree. I grabbed Cacho's bag of grooming gear and took him down to the water faucet in the camping area. I used my cook pot to rinse the sweat from his back, then gave him a drink. The pot was too small to put his nose in, so I tipped it up, and let him drink as if from a cup. Backwash and water ran down my arm, but it felt good on a warm afternoon. Every indication I knew to look for said Cacho was healthy, the bite on his back healing nicely. At precisely that moment, perhaps he was; however, everything—mood, weather, and even health—can change quickly on the trail.

In the middle of the night I heard a loud, frightening sound, a cross between a squeal and a yelp. At first I thought it might be some large carnivorous creature, but became truly alarmed when I realized that Cacho had made the sound. I unzipped my tent fly hastily and struggled out of my bag to find Cacho in the gloom. He stood tied to a tree, but not sleeping. He seemed upset. Suddenly, he screamed again and lashed out with a hind leg.

I had never heard Cacho, or any horse, make such a noise before. It seemed to be an expression of extreme pain. As I watched, his abdomen contracted and cramped, the tightness moving along his belly. He squealed and shot a hind leg out, kicking at the phantom that tormented him. I chewed the cuticle around my fingernails and watched him for about an hour. He yelped and kicked every five or ten minutes. Finally I couldn't stand it anymore.

"Come on, partner, let's see if walkin' around helps."

It seemed to. I had always heard that walking was good for stomach cramps. I walked him for an hour, then tied him to a hitching post. I sat nearby, cold and distressed, in the dirt. After a few minutes, he cried out again.

I led Cacho over to a meadow dotted with tents. I shivered in the wet lawn, wearing my Patagonia jacket but wishing I had my warm sleeping bag to wrap around my shoulders. To my great relief, Cacho grazed quietly. Even so, I considered worst-case scenarios. I had come almost halfway—nearly 700 miles of a 1,500-mile trip. I had come far enough that I could be proud of my accomplishment. Whatever character-building pain and solitude I was going to experience had probably already happened. I could understand J. Smeaton Chase fixing on his goal and trading in his horse to reach it. But if Cacho's colic proved persistent, I might choose a different path.

Eventually the sun crept over the horizon and lit up my spot in the grass, warming me. Three colorful nylon chrysalises situated near me slowly discharged six people yawning and stretching like butterflies. They ignored Cacho and me, made coffee, and brought it to a picnic table. Still wearing slippers and pajamas, they took turns reading aloud from a book. I listened for a while, but as more campers began stirring, I prodded Luke out of his tent, loaded up quickly and got Cacho walking again.

While he was walking, his colic disappeared, but I didn't know how soon it might return. The best thing to do was to find places with hay to put his digestive track back to normal.

As I contemplated the problem, I gave Luke a granola bar and a handful of dried cherries for breakfast. "Dried cherries are my favorite," he said, not complaining. I figured this was especially true when he was starving. I would have provided something more, but that was all I had with me, other than food that required cooking, and I didn't want to take the time. I felt a little guilty for having him come so far to help me, then not providing more in the way of food. He had been invaluable, but already I could reach the straps he'd been helping me secure. There was nothing he could do about Cacho's colic, so when we reached the highway, we parted ways.

⋆⋆⋆

My worries about getting hay to calm Cacho's digestive tract were resolved sooner than I imagined possible, when I ended up at Maggetti Ranch, a place with plenty of hay a where no one was concerned about how long a visitor might stay. It had been described to me as "that cult place, Synanon. Remember the cult that sent the rattlesnake to the lawyer back in the '70s—that place."

Synanon had started as a drug rehabilitation center. In the early years it was a good neighbor. However, as the place began to transition from a drug rehabilitation center treating temporary residents to a permanent religious commune, the neighbors became less enchanted. According to articles in the *Point Reyes Light,* one neighbor alleged that Synanon security forces had ambushed and beaten him for helping runaways. The *Point Reyes Light* was the first, but other news organizations began running unflattering stories, culminating in a Justice Department inquiry into Synanon's investment in weapons. Synanon responded to negative press coverage by leveling libel charges against several journals. In the end, beset by legal expenses, Synanon sold its Marin properties, including Maggetti Ranch, to the Buck Foundation for $6.3 million, and slipped from the news scene.

If I had fallen down the rabbit hole when I arrived in Woodside, I stepped through the looking glass when I arrived at Synanon. An odd mix of old and new buildings littered the gently rolling hills. A stately old Victorian that clearly predated Synanon stood at the entrance to the 1,502-acre ranch. The ornate woodwork was carefully painted in three shades: white, tan, and dark sienna. The yard had a suggestion of order, but weeds dominated the lawn and sprang up through cracks in the concrete walkways. Occasional piles of cow manure indicated that livestock roamed the property.

Cacho joined the foreman's oversized quarter horse in a spacious corral. "Tank" dwarfed little Cacho, but they had similar, calm temperaments. They sniffed each other's nostrils, showing only modest interest. As I leaned on the railing and watched Cacho settle in, the foreman, Rich, joined me. At his heels a spaniel with gentle cinnamon eyes raised its eyebrows as we talked, as if following the conversation. I asked the dog's name.

"This here is Jake." As the Cheshire cat left his grin behind, so those sweet, loving dog eyes lingered even when he lost interest in me, the newcomer, and trotted off on canine business.

"Here, I'll show you where you can put your gear." Rich led me to the barn. "I've got a calf I'm hand rearing. Wanna see it?" We got a bottle for the calf, and opened the door to a pen behind the barn. His gangly little legs brought him at a run to gulp the milk.

"Got some stuff I gotta do in town. Just make yourself at home." I took him up on his invitation to stay a few days. It would give me a chance to provide Cacho hay to cure his colic, and also let the bite on his back heal.

Morning breathed out a wet coastal fog. I found Cacho

and Tank happily munching on alfalfa. Rich's pickup was gone, but brown-and-white Jake wagged his stubby tail in greeting. "Left you alone, huh, buddy?" He shoved his wet nose under my hand. "Going to take Cacho for a walk. Wanna come?" Initially I also extended the invitation to Tank, but he proved to be too much trouble, so I left him behind. He watched us longingly and whinnied once, but decided not to whine about it.

On the road to Synanon —Two couples out enjoying a drive in their classic cars don't know what to think of Cacho socializing with them.
Photo by Lisa Wood

I took Jake and Cacho to some school buildings with broken windows and leaves blown into all the corners. I let Cacho drag his lead line and graze outside while Jake and I explored the rooms. Several articles, such as a *San Francisco Examiner* article from May 23, 1972, described a Synanon uniform of overalls and short haircut. They said the curriculum included learning about the evils of drugs and that their leader was the Messiah. I could imagine rows of well-disciplined young children wearing overalls, learning their lessons, while older children and adults spent long hours manufacturing key chains and ballpoint pens embossed with various company logos to defray the organization's expenses.

Victorian house at Synanon. The resident of the house took the photo for me.

Soon the darkness inside the rooms pushed me outside to a great lattice-covered patio with a classic view across a meadow to rolling hills. I sat on a brick barbecue and imagined picnics here. They would have instilled a sense of community, heightened by the extremely different customs and values of the people. Apparently I dawdled too long, because Jake lost interest and went about his own business.

I spent my days at Synanon relaxing and exploring. I finished a couple of books, and found residents I could leave them with as I prepared to depart. It seemed I had stayed at Synanon for a long time, though it had been only three days.

On the last day, Rich, who had taken his time getting to know me, felt comfortable enough with me to reveal a secret. We were drinking cokes in his dark little bungalow, at a kitchen table littered with crusted empty bean cans and other debris. He had been telling me about riding bulls in rodeos, but there was a lull in the conversation. I filled it by saying, "So I'll be heading on tomorrow morning. Thanks again for everything." There was another pause.

"You're out there for days, alone. What do you do? Don't you get lonely?" he asked softly, dark green eyes glued to his soda can.

"Well, no. I mean, I meet people. And if there aren't any people around, I build a fire or mend my bag that keeps ripping, or read."

"Oh. Keeps you company, reading?"

"Yeah, it's great. It's like I'm in the middle of all the people I'm reading about. Can't get lonely when you're reading."

Rich paused, looking seriously at some crumbs on the cracking vinyl tabletop. His curly brown hair fell across his face, obscuring his dark eyes. "I wouldn't know," he almost whispered. The muscles on his face contracted visibly, casting a forlorn shadow into the hollows of his cheeks.

"Oh. You don't read?"

"No, it's not that." He took a deep breath, closed his lips, and exhaled with a "pff" sound. "I can't." His face flushed, and his tone reflected humiliation.

"It must be tough to get by."

He got his face under control. "I do OK. Most people don't know. I don't usually tell people unless I have to. I guess I'm jealous that you can read. Lotta people seem to think you're stupid if you can't read. I dunno. Maybe I am."

"Yeah, I have to agree with that. Anybody who'd intentionally sit on an angry bull has got to be a little off." I teased. He laughed and took the opportunity to change the subject. (Rich has long since moved on to another ranch, so I feel comfortable that I'm not compromising his secret by telling this story.)

⋆⋆

I managed to get hay for Cacho almost every day, but even so he had another bout of colic. So it was with relief that I accepted an invitation to camp at a stable near Gualala, the southern entry to Mendocino County, and with enthusiasm that I accepted an invitation to join the owners, Pat and Charles, for dinner. Pat asked about my experiences on the trail.

"I tell a story I call 'The Time Cacho Saved My Life,'" I volunteered. "He lost his footing in some shale, and I bailed out of the saddle while he was rearing up on his hind legs. Rather than come down and crush my skull, he veered to the downhill side and sent himself down a gorge."

"Hmm, it's hard to know his motivation. Any horse will try not to get his legs tangled in a fallen rider, so it's hard to say if he was self-sacrificing, or if it was just self-preservation instinct." Pat seemed unconcerned about the distinction.

"Yeah, I know. It was probably a little of both; I do feel protectiveness from him, but I want to be honest." For me to feel authentic in my storytelling, the underlying meaning, the heart of the matter, has to be true.

"I think he *did* save your life." I felt sisterly toward Pat because she shared with me a heroic notion of my animal. Also, she didn't question my description of him as having a good sense of humor. Non-horse people were more skeptical and sometimes demanded an illustration of one of his jokes. I would explain, "There's a game I call the 'Lisa Tip,' where he stops eating grass to nudge me as I sit reading nearby. He does it repeatedly, pushing a little harder each time, only stopping when I tip over and put down my book." I think he thinks that's really funny.

* ★ *

The next day, still, warm, dry air felt delicious after so many days of cold fog. The intensely green trees took no notice when, for the first time in the entire trip, I took off my long-sleeved shirt and rode in my black tank top. Warm rays penetrated my newly exposed skin. Enjoying the blue sky, smelling the woody fragrance of the firs and redwoods, I dismounted to eat some manzanita apples. Why not engage all the senses? They tasted like not very good green apples, but somehow the flavor was perfect in the moment.

Cacho's hooves clattered as he carried me down the mountain, back toward the coast. Near Point Arena the forest gave way to open pastures filled with green grass and wildflowers. Scraps of scrubby, salt-pruned native shrubs huddled near the ground around the perimeters of pastures. The small, windswept town did not boast distinctive architecture, but it did have a scenic lighthouse.

I found Saint Aloysius church; a single-story stucco building painted a particularly unattractive institutional green. The priest knew I was coming and was expecting me. I had stayed on the property of members of his flock down the coast for the last few days, including Pat and Charles. My progress seemed incredibly slow to him and to other church members who had, I learned, been awaiting my arrival for days. News of my unusual travels had spread up the coast much more quickly than Cacho could carry me; apparently a degree of anticipation had built. "You must hurry to town," he urged. "Some people are waiting for you."

In town I was greeted by a handmade banner proclaiming WELCOME LISA WOOD AND COTCHO! One person gave me a silk rose, and several others joined in to welcome me royally. Flustered, I fumbled for words, but enjoyed being such a celebrity.

A warm welcome at Point Arena

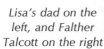

Lisa's dad on the left, and Falther Talcott on the right

* ★ *

Morning brought bone-chilling, wet, foggy weather, turning the landscape bleak and gray. I trekked the side of the seldom-traveled road in miserably cold solitude. The heavy, swirling mists blotted out the broad valley of the Garcia River. Unlike some fogs, which seem to provide companionship in their texture and personality, this soulless fog only cut me off from the surroundings. Cacho also seemed to withdraw into his own thoughts.

I was feeling dramatically hard-bitten when a car pulled onto the shoulder ahead of me. The driver rolled down her window and asked, "Are you Dorothy Wood's daughter? She told me her daughter would be riding up this way. My goodness, dear, how far have you come, from San Diego?"

"No, I started in Los Angeles," I sniffed, my nose running, but my attitude warmed by her greeting. Hard to feel lost in the elements when someone is calling you "dear." She wished me well, and I continued on, feeling less lonely despite the desolate day.

My destination was a minuscule town named Elk. Previously known as Greenwood, Elk perched on a bluff above the sea, just a bit short of twenty miles north of Point Arena. Nestled between a mile-long beach and a forest of redwoods and cedars, this town of 200 had been a prosperous port city of 2,000 before the stock market crash of 1929 helped drive out the lumber industry, and subsequent fires destroyed many landmarks. Cacho and I received a warm welcome from another parishioner in Elk, but the next day's accommodations would prove surprisingly difficult, especially considering that I had made arrangements in advance. Ugh, the nerve-wracking, daily struggle to find a place to stay.

What happened was that the rangers at Van Damme State Park, a scenic park located just south of Fort Bragg, reneged on the agreement we had made by phone for me to camp there. Digging in their heels, they insisted it was "too dangerous" for me to camp there with a horse. Reluctantly, I led my falsely accused partner on, worried about *our* safety. I searched for a generous soul with private land, having been rejected on public land.

The sun dissolved behind the omnipresent fog bank over the waters of the Pacific. In the gathering gloom, Cacho eyed every gate and pasture hopefully, but nothing appropriate presented itself.

Somebody had mentioned that I might be welcomed by people with a surname similar to mine, but I couldn't quite remember the name. With great hope and wishful thinking, I decided to inquire at a house with the surname "Woody" prominently displayed on the mailbox. The front portion of the half-acre lot had been allowed to go wild, and had a decent amount of weedy grass and a couple of trees. The house itself, built in the eighties, with dark wooden lines, and a well-tended yard around it, looked large and comfortable.

I left Cacho in the gravel drive and climbed a couple of steps to knock on the door. When a middle-aged woman with a compassionate face answered, I surprised her by blurting out, "Um, hi, could you step out here and talk with me? See, I left my horse untied in your driveway." I backed down the stairs, and amazingly, the woman followed me, no sign of fear on her face, only curiosity.

"Oh, yes, I see you have," she said as we descended the steps. Whatever menace the rangers had seen in us was invisible to her, and she warmly invited us to stay on her property.

* * *

On the way to Fort Bragg I had a thrilling, climactic encounter with my ever-present nemesis: that fiend named Traffic.

It seemed surprising that it should wait until I had made my way to the remote part of the state rather than attacking right at the beginning, in more populous southern California. But it had been saving its strength and growing larger. When my moment to face it arrived, it came in the shape of a heavily loaded logging truck. The narrow road was twisted with turns, and on the steep uphill the driver downshifted noisily, making his truck roar like the monster it truly was. To give me more room would put his beast squarely in the path of oncoming traffic. I would have fled in terror, but a steep embankment forced me to hold my ground, and again my noble, unshakable mount did not let me down. With inches to spare we lived to remember the battle—though it took awhile to get my pulse back to double digits.

Though it wasn't exactly the Holy Grail, in Fort Bragg I found the building where I was born: my reward for having faced the traffic dragon. I photographed Cacho in front of the structure before retreating from the town to a trail that ran along the beach. Winding through a wooded park, the path became dusty and strewn with manure, a sure sign of a nearby stable. I came upon large groups of riders on fat, irascible-but-gentle, horses. The trail traversed the highway at a well-marked equestrian crossing. The stable featured a tremendous barn, a dusty yard lined with halter-strewn hitching posts, and three or four corrals filled with dozens of horses.

Sweet-smelling sawdust covered the barn floor, and bales of clean straw were arranged in the wide center aisle for convenient seating or for parking a saddle. Jodhpur-clad equestrians led horses here and there, creating a constant level of activity. No one paid any particular attention to me. I unsaddled Cacho and led him around, trying to find out where we belonged.

I found a wrangler and explained my travels. I said I thought I had permission to stay.

"Oh, *you're* the one." He put his mangled, well-chewed pencil down and stood up, looking at me appraisingly like a horse buyer at an auction. "Sure, yeah, just a minute and I'll show you where you can put him." The lanky, weather-beaten man finished writing something down, closed the pages of the notebook and said, "So you're going from Mexico to Canada. You traveling alone?"

People often assumed my travels extended that far; I had stopped correcting them. "No, Cacho is with me," I said, rubbing Cacho's broad forehead affectionately. He liked the caress and pushed back, threatening to throw me off balance. Some people had seemed annoyed by my oft-re-peated response to the often-asked question, but the wrangler's lips curled up. He understood what I was really saying.

"That's not what I meant, but yeah, I reckon it does make a difference, doesn't it? He seems like a friendly fella." He petted Cacho's honey-colored mane with the slow, firm motion of someone comfortable around horses. Cacho's head dropped in appreciation.

The wrangler cast his eyes over my pile of trail-worn possessions. "That a military saddle? No padding. People either like them or they hate them. It's a good saddle, but kinda hard." He wasn't the kind of man to make long speeches. "You know, I used to be a cement mixer; made darned good money, too, but working with horses, that's what I like, and my wife is OK with it, even if I make less money." My heart skipped a beat at this man's understated under-standing. He realized the difficulties of my adventure, but also the rewards.

* ⋆ *

Leaving the stable in the chilly, overcast morning, we clattered through a prosperous residential area of attractive wooden houses nestled into large lots with tall trees and green, well-kept lawns. We clomped down the sidewalk and then, more quietly, Cacho's hooves digging into the sand, out onto MacKerricher State Beach. A gentle breeze drifted across the foamy surf, and I inhaled its brisk, salty freshness. Clear, well-traveled trails petered out, and soon Cacho labored through deep, untraveled strand. People often asked me if he enjoyed traveling. He seemed to, but his favorite thing was looking for places with rich, tender grass. His head low, Cacho zigzagged his way up the unvegetated beach as if clinically depressed, unexcited about making forward progress in this inedible zone.

After a few miles Cacho brought me to the firm footing of the road along Mill Creek, and we left the dunes. His attitude improved markedly. He noted an abundance of grass, and I noted a scenic landscape. Viewed along the periscope of Cacho's neck and framed by his furry ears, the road ran along the north bank of a beautiful estuary, characterized by low, uniformly even, thick, deep-green vegetation. A languid watercourse wound its way through the marsh, in no hurry to get to the ocean. At low tides the river ran to the sea, but at high tides the salty seawater came inland to greet the freshwater stream. Cacho moved like that river, in no particular hurry. I noted the low, graceful hills on the far bank of the estuary. The waterway reflected the hills, mirroring their tall shrubs as if thinking about them. Snowy white egrets, brown and green ducks and a multitude of smaller birds floated on the water, waded in the channels and flitted among the banks.

Two young boys, about seven or eight years old, pedaled up the dirt road behind me. "Afternoon," I said. One of them mumbled something that might have been a shy greeting, and then they bicycled quickly past me. They stood on their pedals, pushing their small bikes violently from side to side as they raced. Even after they turned a corner, I could hear them up ahead, shouting and competing with each other.

A soft, overcast afternoon light illuminated a dilapidated Victorian house. I sat down nearby on a patch of scraggly grass to rest and eat a granola bar, and soon the two boys rode back over. They pointed out a herd of elk grazing in the estuary. I admired the elk and, in return, I showed them a garter snake I had noticed in the grass. "You staying here?" one of them asked.

"Yes, just for the night. My name is Lisa." A woman driving a Chrysler had stopped me two days earlier and invited me here. I described her, and asked the boys if they knew her.

"No, but there's lots of people here. We live up on the hill there." I saw a small house. A woman stepped outside the front door. As I watched, the jeans-clad figure put her fingers to her lips and whistled. "Gotta go," one of the boys said.

Eventually I found the Chrysler driver, and she directed me to where I could stay. Cacho shared an enclosure with a pugnacious goat. The little animal out-toughed Cacho for a pile of oats I gathered. "Good night, Cacho. Don't let Butt-Head get you."

The next day an equestrian neighbor named Nancy (not the same Nancy who had provided hospitality near Monterey) arrived astride a hot-blooded gray stallion whose short rein had whipped the sweat on his neck into a froth. A friend on a less troublesome, bloodstone-colored mare accompanied

Nancy. They offered to show me a route I could use to avoid the highway. Both rode on tidy English saddles, holding tightly to delicate leather reins, and directing their horses as nobility might command a servant.

"Keep a distance from the stallion," the middle-aged, dark-haired equestrian instructed sharply. "Don't let the reins lie so slack."

I legged Cacho over, giving the stallion even more room. Seeing my reins still loose on Cacho's neck, she pushed her point. "It's important to maintain contact. Pull his head in until it is perpendicular to the ground. It's all about form." Chastened and criticized, I held the reins, but I stubbornly continued to keep them slack. I didn't care if Cacho held his head low and led with his nose, as long as he got me safely where I wanted to go. The heat of resentment toward the woman's arrogant tone welled up in me.

"So, where does this road come out? At Highway 1?" I asked, trying to keep the conversation away from riding style.

"No, but it'll be easy to get there. We will drop you at the trail. It's an old logging road. Just stay to the right and the logging road will take you west to Highway 1."

When Nancy left us at the trailhead, I signaled Cacho up the hill that she'd said would take me through the forest and back to the highway. Cacho moved aggressively, as if he were as happy as I was to leave the company of that critical woman. He trotted past towering trees and their under-story of ripe raspberries. At the crest, we came to an intersection of neglected dirt roads, marked in the middle with a large pile of seedy bear scat, like a road sign. I nudged Cacho to the right. I was still confident, but was beginning to wonder if the woman had any personal knowledge of the trail.

The trail narrowed until at last it disintegrated into a tangle of new growth. At first Cacho threaded his way easily though the small young shrubs and pine saplings, but further on the forest had reclaimed the road. The trees grew close to each other, competing to see who could grow tallest the fastest. I dismounted, leading Cacho through the maze of branches. Having committed myself to at least fifteen miles in this direction, I felt reluctant to turn back. Forward motion can be a seductive siren, and I had fallen under her hypnotic spell.

Cacho obligingly ducked under an overhanging limb while simultaneously stepping over a low branch. He stopped when a branch pressed upon the wither bags. I lifted it so he could take another step, but then a limb pressed against the bedroll. A foot at a time we played a game of *Twister*, literally picking our way through a three-dimensional labyrinth. I sensed our proximity to the sea, probably less than five miles to the west, and felt drawn to it, but eventually I realized I could spend days struggling through what might be an impenetrable barrier.

I retraced our way through the vegetation, and then, faced with a maze of dead-end trails, began to wonder if I could find my way back to the road. As all scouts know, there are two options in such a situation: 1) Calmly assess the options, and make prudent decisions on trails based on the best possible information; and 2) Panic. Although the latter might be emotionally rewarding, Cacho's dependency on my guidance made me select the former.

The sun sagged in the western sky as I attempted to retrace our steps, so speed was necessary to reach a place that had grass and water—Cacho's camping requirements. I urged Cacho into a canter at every level and uphill spot, and encouraged a rapid walk or sometimes a trot on the downhills. There was neither fodder nor water under the dense, tall trees. The friendly whisper of a breeze in the boughs helped me hold my fears at bay as I concentrated on the twists and turns of the trail, trying to remember which fork I had taken at each intersection. I smiled when we passed the bear scat, sure of the turn.

I felt angry with myself for being so foolish. I reminded myself of my rule: Never take someone's advice about a trail unless you're sure the person has traveled the trail. *Himself. This year. On a horse.*

A surveyor had set up his equipment at the place where the women had left me. Stopping Cacho, I greeted the man.

"Howdy," he returned my greeting.

"Say, just wondering, do any of these old logging roads go through to Highway 1?" I pointed back the way I had come.

"Hmm, no, I don't think so. I don't think any of 'em ever did, even originally. Pretty sure none of 'em do now." Given his occupation, he should know. "You with the horse camp?" he asked.

"I'm sorry, what horse camp?" I inquired, very interested.

"It's just up the road here. If you turn left when you get to the pavement you can't miss it. I figured you were from it."

I followed his directions, and there, as he said, a horse camp filled a large meadow with horses, mules, trucks, trailers, portable fences, RVs and lawn chairs. What a feast for my tired, worried eyes.

I unloaded my story on the first person I saw, who fortunately turned out to be a compassionate listener named Valerie. She responded sympathetically to my story of the forest imbroglio and invited me to camp with her.

Soon I was relaxing, sipping iced tea, and feeling trouble-free. We watched some of the more macho members of the equestrian club cantering their horses through the meadow. "Bet they don't ride their horses more than twice a year," Valerie speculated. We overheard snippets of conversation from these cowboys. On the equestrian club's annual camp-out, many of them had ridden eight or ten miles in the last day or two, and they were suffering for it. We heard comments like, "My butt is so sore I'm gonna need a sling." and "Man, I gotta get some more beer or my ass is gonna kill me."

"I'm riding my butt off," one man shouted to another as they thundered by on a fast, attention-grabbing gallop. The two men rushed back thirty minutes later to get in their 4x4s and go to town to get more beer.

"So much for riding his rear off," Valerie laughed.

The next morning I found a resident veterinarian at the horse camp. She was a thin woman about my own age, and wore her long brown hair pulled back in a single braid.

"Could you check out my horse and see how he's holding up?" I asked, after explaining the extent of my travels.

"Well, sure, but I'd have to charge you," she replied.

I had recently been to an ATM machine, so that was no problem. "He's holding his weight, even putting some on, but he has had a touch of colic and his eyes are a little red. I've been grooming him every day, and maybe I gave him an infection with bacteria from my hand."

"Well, bring him over here. I'm almost done with this one," she said, concentrating on her current patient, bending close to a leg wound on a large black mule.

I returned shortly with Cacho. She looked at him and said he looked remarkably good, but yes, a mild infection reddened his eyes. "Appies are notorious for eye infections," she told me. "It's all the white part around the eye. It's not bad, but I think it should be treated. How gentle is he?"

"He's a lamb," I assured her.

"OK, we have to clean out the tear ducts. I'll just try, and see if he'll let me do it."

Cleaning out the tear ducts meant flushing them with saline, which entailed shoving a large tube up each nostril. Or, I should say, *attempting* to shove a tube up his nostrils. Cacho saw the tubes coming and immediately tried to kill the vet. For such an easygoing animal, he suddenly became more than just stubborn; he actually tried to turn his tail to her so he could send her to southern California with his powerful hindquarters. She stood back respectfully, and called her husband over to help her. "Twitch him for me, will you?"

"Where do you want him twitched, the lip or the ear?" the muscular man asked her.

"Whatever you think will work," she said. I stood holding his lead rope, not liking what was going on, but understanding that, given Cacho's behavior, she had to protect herself.

The strong man twisted Cacho's upper lip tightly in a chain with a long wooden handle to get his attention and distract him. When Cacho tried to toss his head, he twisted harder, inflicting pain, which Cacho ignored, yanking his head from the man's grip. Once free, Cacho backed away from the two people. He had a wary look on his face, but let me grab his lead rope and lead him back. "Really," I said sheepishly, "he is normally a lamb."

She turned her back to me and rummaged in a cabinet mounted in the bed of her pickup. "OK, well, I'm going to have to tranq him."

"Can I ride him later if you tranquilize him?"

"Yeah, it'll wear off in a couple of hours. He may be a little mellow though. Just stand by his head there. Good.

Hold his halter while I—well, my, he doesn't seem to mind shots."

* * *

Mellow does not begin to describe the purple haze of a trance in which Cacho carried me to our campsite in Deltahaven. By the time we arrived, though, he was feeling quite energetic. Also, he apparently did not feel dependent on my company. With a delicious meadow for a campsite, I thought he'd find enough grass to keep him happy. Not suspecting his shenanigans, I shucked my footwear and got out a book, but he was not content to leave me to my leisure, he decided to make his break for it.

He trotted past me and headed purposefully down the road. I gave chase, running barefoot through the glade. The grass was cool and soft; as soon as I got to the road, however, I regretted the nakedness of my feet. The jagged, irregular rocks of the gravel road pounded into my soles with each stride. I had to ignore the cutting and bruising and catch Cacho. If he made it to the end of Deltahaven Road before I did, he would encounter Highway 1. I imagined him turning south and heading back to San Diego. Mustangs don't live very long, I thought to myself, picturing a truck slamming into his body.

Cacho had a jolly time playing his little game of keep-away. When I walked, he walked. If I stopped and turned back to the meadow, he continued on as if he didn't need me. I cursed his remarkably independent spirit. If I jogged to close the gap between us, he watched me with his excellent peripheral vision and let me gain a little, but kept me thoroughly out of reach. I pretended I didn't care, trying to look like I was concentrating on other things, not playing his game, as I hobbled painfully down the street.

Then I heard it. The sound of my salvation: a truck engine approaching from behind. This would change the rules of Cacho's game.

A woman, mid-thirties, whose noticeably attractive features, strong bones and long black hair clearly proclaimed Native-American heritage, approached from behind me, driving an old red pickup. I *had* to make her stop, or Cacho was lost. I turned toward the oncoming truck, stepping firmly into its path, and held up my hand.

I don't know how much of the situation she understood, but she slowed without blinking, almost as if she were expecting me. As I hopped in, I said, "Oh, my gosh, you have great timing. That's my horse striking out on his own there, and if you could please just ease past him and let me out on the other side of him, I'll intercept him with no problem."

"Sure thing," she said with a nod, pleasantly, but with no desire for chitchat. She kept her eyes steady, glued to the road in front of her. Expertly, she eased past Cacho and dropped me just the right distance in front of him to prepare for the catch. She drove on without pausing to see if I was successful.

Once in position ahead of him, I had no worries. As I predicted, he walked right up to me, making no effort at evasion. The game had been the chase, and once I stood in front of him, the game was over.

"Bad boy," I scolded, once his lead line rested safely in my hand. I turned to take him back up the road. Suddenly I became acutely aware of how sharp the stones really were. I thought about swinging up onto him and using the halter as a bridle. Pushing off against the cutting edges would not be a welcome exercise. As I contemplated the move, a woman appeared on the road, strolling toward me, a pair of sandals dangling casually from one hand. I stood my ground and waited for her.

She introduced herself, saying, "I saw you go running past the window of my trailer barefoot, and thought you might need these."

Angels. Out of nowhere. A saving grace.

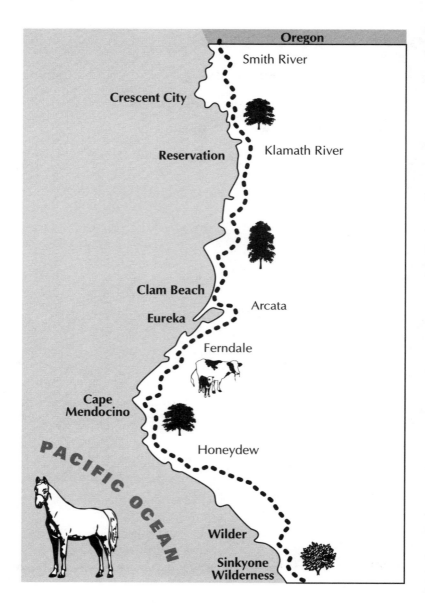

Map 5

5

Reaching a Decision

The angel who saved my feet from the ravages of the stones also gave me directions to the wilderness area I planned to visit next. Despite her detailed directions, I managed somehow to miss the turn. After about thirteen miles, the road turned inland and was swallowed by the heavy forest of Hales Grove. Weary, I wanted to call it a day, but there were no creeks or grassy turnouts. I decided the first reasonable camping spot would be the end of the day's travels, no matter what. Cacho plodded on another five miles, but we found no suitable spot for camping. I adjusted my campsite standards accordingly.

Finally, I saw a break in the grass-suppressing forest. As I neared, I saw that the reason for the clear spot was a house with a big yard and a bit of grass. Gratefully, I turned up the driveway, sure that I could talk the residents into allowing me to camp. A gangly, preadolescent German-shepherd-blend dog growled and barked at us.

"I'll just make myself comfortable while I wait for your owners," I said conversationally to the pup. He responded in silence, his oversized ears perked, one of them flopping over slightly as if asking a question. He tilted his head and watched intently as I unsaddled Cacho and gave him a drink of water from the dog dish, refilling it from the hose. I moseyed to the porch, which was cluttered with a refrigerator, a dryer, and a few plastic toddler toys in bright, primary colors. I tested the dryer. It worked. There hadn't been an opportunity to do laundry in almost a week, and I was desperate to at least rinse out my socks; the dryer meant I could do so and have fresh, dry socks even in this cool, moist climate.

I cringed with guilt about using the dryer, and furtively checked the socks regularly in hopes of getting them out before I got caught.

In the yard, I inspected a canvas tent. A cot with a child-size sleeping bag was set up inside, and a fan stood near the door, with a long extension cord running to the house.

"Elementary, my dear Watson," I said to the dog, as I deduced that the family had at least two children: the younger one played with the toys on the porch, and the older one played both day and night in this tent.

I put my things in the tent, then spent the rest of the evening helping Cacho find bits of grass. There wasn't much, but more than there'd been on the miles of bare forest ground. When he'd had enough I tied him to a tree and retired to the tent, zipping Watson, the dog, outside. I used the child's cot and my own sleeping bag, and felt very much like Goldilocks helping herself to the belongings of others. I slept fitfully, expecting a flashlight in my face and a frightened, maybe angry, family to send me scurrying into the woods. However, at the early light of dawn it occurred to me that the family must be out of town, probably vacationing somewhere.

Coming here had been an accident; I had missed the turn to Usal and had come almost as far as the next town, Leggett.

Using garden tools that were leaning against the chain link, I cleaned up Cacho's manure and put it all in a wheelbarrow for convenient use in the garden—a little calling card to mark my visit.

Having no tent to dry and pack, we were on the road by 6 A.M. of a gray, misty morning, retracing the steps of the previous day. I breathed a sigh of relief that Cacho and I hadn't been caught trespassing, and beamed at Watson tagging along at my heels. He would turn back before long, I was sure. My only concern was that Cacho had had a skimpy breakfast, having eaten most of the weeds the previous night. I vowed to stop at the first nice clearing we found.

After a couple of miles, I began suggesting to the puppy that he go home. He stared back with loyal eyes. In my sternest voice, I barked at him to beat it. He put his head down and looked up at me with a hangdog expression, but kept on. Eventually, I had to face it: the dog was coming with me into the Lost Coast Wilderness. I figured I'd have to call my parents when I came to a pay phone—which could be days or even weeks—and they would come and take him home. So like Dorothy in Oz, I accepted the tagalong.

* * *

The very word, *wilderness,* evoked a primordial image of wild land; a dark, thick wood where gleaming, carnivorous eyes peered out of the shadows. But, as Roderick Nash put it, "...wilderness is a condition of the mind—a perceived rather than actual condition of the environment..."

There was plenty of evidence of human activity in this wilderness. Riding up the rutted, dusty dirt road, I noted stately trees, but there were also huge stumps scattered across the forest floor, suggesting that at least some of the trees had been logged. Europeans never settled in heavy numbers, but Chase found a few ranches and even hotels in this rugged country in 1911. The extreme topography protected some pockets of magnificent groves from the logger's ax. One of the last surviving old-growth redwood groves was named the J. Smeaton Chase Grove, in honor of the man who inspired my trip and wrote eloquently of the glories of the forest.

The nearby Sally Bell Grove was named in honor of one of the last surviving full-blooded Sinkyone Indians living here. Sally Bell's dramatic story, recorded in G. A. Nomland's *Sinkyone Notes 1935,* reads as follows:

> Soon, about ten o'clock in the morning, some white men came. They killed my grandfather and my mother and my father. I saw them do it. I was a big girl at the time. They killed my baby sister and cut her heart out and threw it into the brush where I ran and hid. My little sister was a baby, just crawling around. I didn't know what to do. I was so scared I guess I just hid there a long time with my little sister's heart in my hands.

Sally Bell survived. And the trees that bear her name will live longer still, whispering their secrets as the wind stirs in their bows. Preserved in this island of "wilderness," the old-growth trees will endure after other forests have been logged, just as Sally lived beyond the massacre of her family.

The sound of an engine interrupted my musings, and I prevailed upon the driver to take Watson home. We had to tie him in to keep him from vaulting out and joining me on my adventure through the wilderness.

The sun struggled to penetrate a thin fog. Gentle lighting made the woods seem mystical; almost supernatural. Bracken ferns and blackberries grew between the rocks and trees on the forest floor. Massive brown tree trunks lifted the eye to the thick green canopy above.

I spent two days in the wilderness with Cacho. Though uplifted by the scenery, worry for Cacho troubled me. His colic grew worse on the sparse grass eking out an existence under the huge trees. We headed toward a place in Kaluna Cliffs, an inroad of settlement in the wilderness, where I hoped I could find accommodations for Cacho. I had come to a decision: I would not finish the trip if Cacho didn't. It was hard to face because we'd come so far, and we had, relatively speaking, so little distance left to go. I hoped this wouldn't be the end of the road, but unless I could keep Cacho healthy, it was over.

Lisa has Cacho's attention - that's an apple behind her back.

Kaluna Cliffs —
Photos by
Merle Wood
(Lisa's dad).

* ⋆ ✶

When we arrived at Kaluna Cliffs the fog was so thick that visibility was no more than twenty feet. From what little I could see, magnificent fir trees stood watch over a few campsites, each with a picnic table and barbecue. Beyond the campsites were a few (empty) horse stalls. Just past these square equestrian accommodations was a large fenced area enclosing dozens of acres, where the proprietors apparently lived in a small travel trailer.

Before I could get my food and stove out of the packs,

Cacho attracted the attention of a beautiful ginger Fjord mare, with a dark mane and tail. The buckskin was a draft horse by confirmation, but no taller than little Cacho. She approached from the fenced yard and whinnied a welcome. Cacho ignored the conversation of his own kind and focused on eating. Hearing the noise, a woman stepped out of the trailer and, seeing me, moved through the mists to stand next to the mare.

"Can I help you with something?" she asked without smiling, her body movements slow and stiff. She looked to be younger than her movements suggested, perhaps in her early forties.

"Hi. I'm Lisa," I said, awkwardly. Desperately hungry and not thinking clearly, I blurted out an incoherent stream of incongruous information. "A man said he thought I could stay here. We've had a tough time the last couple of days. My horse is a little colicky, so I hope it's OK."

"There are campsites over there." The woman interrupted, telling me the price she charged. I had become so accustomed to the kindness of strangers that her rigid manner and focus on fees surprised me.

"Sure, of course. Do I pay now? Can I buy some feed?"

"No, we don't have any extra feed, but you're welcome to let your horse graze. We'll take care of your camp fees later." Her manner was cool and distant, but she made a courteous suggestion regarding the nicest campsite.

"OK. Thank you," I said to her retreating figure. I boiled water immediately, and ripped into a package of dehydrated soup. I burned my tongue, so famished I couldn't wait for the hard vegetables to soak.

Too cold to sit still, I paced while Cacho ripped at a few oat stalks. A stiff breeze picked up and blew the fog around in ghostly wisps. Arms folded, I hid my runny nose in the neck of my jacket, clenching my teeth to keep them from chattering. When Cacho lost interest in grazing, I put him in a stall, latched the gate and, though it was still early, got out of the bluster by crawling into my tent.

The tempest whipped the rain fly noisily. Inside, I nestled into my warm nylon bag. Outside, protective trees watched over me, sheltering my little tent perched on a promontory in a lonesome wilderness by the ocean. I flipped on my fluorescent lantern and opened *Jurassic Park,* the last paperback someone had given me. A flying dinosaur was swooping down at the people. Mr. Crichton described the sound of the wings as that of a tent flapping on a stormy night. I snuggled further into my bag, enjoying the coincidence, as if telling spooky stories around a campfire. When at last I put the book down, I slept well—until Cacho awoke me with his scream of pain.

I slept with my clothes on, so I bolted without delay from the tent in my stocking feet. In the dim, predawn light I saw that his intestines were still cramping. The feed differed too much from one night to the next—dry and then wet. Horses have fairly touchy digestive systems; they need regular conditions, and they can die from colic. Dietary change is surprisingly difficult for them to handle. I led him around and then let him graze, which seemed to settle his stomach, but the fix was temporary. I had to do something more. Somehow the feed had to be more regular.

The initial frostiness of my hostess, Pam, melted, and she invited me to use her satellite phone to deal with Cacho's health emergency. She said I must wait until later in the day, when the reception was better. At the agreed-upon time, I went to the trailer and used the phone while she and her husband and two sons watched in deep concern. I made arrangements for my parents to bring me my car so that I could use it to stash hay at intervals up the coast to provide Cacho consistent fodder.

"Lucky you found people with a phone," Dad said.

"Is there anything we can do for them? Should we bring groceries?" Mom asked, static prickling the connection.

"That's a good idea. It's a long drive to anywhere. Also, they're low on hay, so if you wouldn't mind bringing some, that would be great." I thanked them and said good-bye, looking up from the receiver to see the intent faces of Pam and her family.

"Just like that, your parents are going to drop everything and drive hundreds of miles over winding dirt roads?" Pam asked, amazed.

"Yeah, of course." I shrugged. I took my parents' support for granted. "They can't come for a couple of days, though, so if it would be all right I'd like to stay a little longer." By staying in one place, I could provide consistent grazing areas and probably keep the colic under control.

"Hmm. Since you're going to be here for a couple of days, would you like to go to a potluck with us?" She asked. "It's in honor of the sheriff's retirement, and most of the community will be there. I'm sure you would be welcome."

* * *

I had exactly three sets of clothes with me: my shorts and a tank top; ever-so-stylish stretch pants and a pearl-buttoned black shirt; and my daily riding wear—jeans and a heavy-duty, forest green shirt. With these fashions to choose from, I selected my green stretch pants and black shirt, topped off with my purple *Patagonia* jacket.

Several elderly women attended the tables, which were laden with heavy dishes of homemade foods: berry pies, home-baked bread, baked salmon, and homegrown vegetables. It was the most spectacular potluck I had ever attended, and

I heaped my plate three times.

As I picked at the buttery, cinnamon-coated piecrust on a raspberry-apple pie, a woman sat down at the old upright piano. She worked her arthritis-afflicted fingers over the keys, leading us in a number of hymns. Then the ceremony honoring the sheriff began. One by one, the elderly residents, and the occasional younger ones, got up and gave tribute.

One woman, in her seventies, a spare figure, slightly hunched over with age, rose to tell her story. Affection for nature brought her to this remote outpost. She loved the trees and all the creatures that lived in them, so early one Sunday morning when she was driving along a dirt road and encountered a snake, she wanted to be sure she didn't hurt it. The animal was stretched across the road, enjoying the sun, and it wouldn't move out of her way. She stopped and got out, using her jacket to "shoo" the snake away. It responded by sinking its fangs into her wrap and refusing to let go.

She put her car in reverse until she found a place where she could turn around and drive to the sheriff's house. Still in his nightclothes, he put on his robe and boots and followed her to where the snake had taken her jacket. There he found her jacket in a ditch, but no sign of the culprit. As she finished her story, she concluded that even "thieving snakes" knew to make themselves scarce around such an excellent officer.

* * *

Two days later, as arranged, my parents brought my car. Although I had experienced much kindness from people in my travels, it was good to see two who knew me so well.

They knew my concern about Cacho, and they also knew about my private tribulation. They asked about my friends, Susan and Derek, and I told them what I had learned the last time I had used a pay phone to call San Diego. Their baby, Jory, was alive but in a coma. He was expected to live another month. Assuming I could get Cacho's colic under control, I would be back home before he died.

Driving seemed strange and unnatural. I bounced along the bumpy dirt road in spectacular sunshine. After spending so much time traveling slowly, 10 MPH seemed like the Indy 500. The scenery flipped by too fast to smell or touch or even really see.

My mission was successful. I found people who agreed to let me stash hay for Cacho, but I hit a snag in the Redwood Campground area. The state park ranger thought the national park could handle my situation, and the national park ranger thought the state park would best handle it. As the parks were side by side, either one would do, if I could just get them to stop ping-ponging me back and forth. Ultimately, the buck stopped at the national park, and I stashed some hay in a barn on park property. I zipped off down the highway, traveling at what seemed like blinding speeds on the broad, sunlit road.

My parents met me again, collected my car, and wished me well on the last leg of my journey. It felt good to be back with Cacho. Ah, now I was on vacation. The weighty concerns about finding good fodder and a safe place to camp were gone. I had made arrangements from Kaluna Cliffs to the border. Now I was really on holiday. The hard part, I was sure, was completely finished.

* ⁎ *

At Wilder Ridge, I left the wilderness area and, coincidentally, devoured the most luscious meal of my life. Perhaps part of the reason it was so distinctly delectable was because of a stark comparison to a ghastly eating experience earlier. I don't want to embarrass anyone, so I will keep the location of that nasty dinner to myself. This disaster began as a generous invitation; no hint of the nauseating details. At the door, it was not the aroma of food that greeted me. At first I couldn't place the odor. I had never smelled anything like it. It was overpowering. My hostess, her large body enveloped by a dirty easy chair, a cast on her foot, held a dachshund in her lap. The animal had milky eyes and an unhealthy coat.

"Poor little thing can't even see. Can barely walk. He never goes outside any more. He's my little precious, though." She squeaked the last sentence in falsetto.

I realized what the smell was. Against the wall, some newspapers had been put out for the dog to use as his toilet. The papers hadn't been changed in a very long time—perhaps since the woman hurt her foot, or maybe even before that.

"Well, let me get dinner ready." The woman carefully set the dog on the worn, dirty carpeting and hefted herself out of the chair. Leaning on the furniture, she limped around the counter that separated the living room area from the kitchen.

"The bread's stale, but I know this great trick. A little steam fixes stale bread up just great." She prepared some sad zucchini, stale bread, and beans with hamburger, all in a rusty old electric skillet. She stirred the colorless lump of food. "Well, dinner's ready, help yourself."

The woman took a large helping for herself, holding the wooden dish with one hand and the counter with the other.

"Can I help you?" I asked as she carried her dinner awkwardly to her easy chair.

"No, I got it." She made it to the chair and plopped down heavily with a grunt. Each time she moved, the chair complained with a screech.

I eased into a brownish-green overstuffed chair across from her, took a spoon and studied the glob in my bowl. I said to myself, "This has carbohydrates, proteins and fats. You need these things. This is nutrition. You've had a long day and need calories." And with that pep talk, I brought a spoonful to my lips. Unfortunately, my stomach hadn't been listening to my mind. It had been paying attention to the wretched signals from my nose. Upon placing the food in my mouth, I gagged immediately.

Frantically, I wondered what Miss Manners would do in such a situation. I had just visibly retched over this kind woman's food. Befuddled, I blurted a lie: "I'm sorry, I've had a little stomach trouble."

"Oh, I have some Pepto, shall I get it?"

"No, I think I should just go lie down for a while." I made a hasty exit, and ate a granola bar as I curled up in my nylon bag.

Yuck! Talk about making camp food seem good by comparison! So, when I arrived at Wilder Ridge and had such an outstanding meal, I was eternally grateful to find food so savory it could drive out the memory of that foul fare. As horrible as the bad meal had been, the good one was exceedingly more delicious. Again, the invitation to dinner included no harbinger of the coming experience, which I describe with relish.

The sound of Mick Jagger on a radio led me up the stairs to the front door, which stood open, though the screen door was closed. I peered inside through the gray haze of the mesh.

On one side of the door was a kitchen, and on the other a dining area open to a large living room. A fantastic view across the valley and to the forested mountains filled the floor-to-ceiling living room windows. Children's toys, and bits of clothing belonging to children and adults, littered the hardwood floors. My hostess greeted me through the screen:

"Ah, you made it," she said, shoving an ice chest toward the door with her foot, and wiping flour from her hands on some skimpy, tight-fitting, cutoff shorts. She wore a snug crop-top shirt, her ample bosom spilling out the top. Her thick blond hair had largely escaped from a plastic clip. Her overall appearance, voluptuous and barefoot, reminded me of the cartoon character "Daisy Mae;" her real name was Sherrie. A ruckus erupted in the living room behind her as two towheaded toddlers jumped on the sofa and screamed at each other in excitement.

Sherrie seemed not to hear the commotion and said, "Your hay is still in the garage." She had to yell to be heard over the children's shrieks and the static-ridden rock-and-roll from a boom box. She stepped onto the porch with me. "Could you grab the other end of this and help me haul it outside?" Sherrie reached down and lifted one side of the ice chest with great ease though it contained a hefty, freshly caught salmon, which she invited me to join in eating. Suddenly, still holding her end of the ice chest, she scowled and yelled, "Hey, kids, knock it off." The corresponding pause in the bedlam lasted a nanosecond, then returned to its former enthusiastic level. "Hey, you two!" she yelled, when the decibel level had reached a particularly intense point, "Go outside and pick some peas, salad stuff and berries for dinner." Then, with renewed vigor, she hollered to her mate, "I'm sending the kids out to pick vegetables."

While chatting with me, Sherrie cooked as if she weren't

paying any attention to the task, yet her biscuits were light and fluffy and her piecrust flaky. Quickly and expertly, she worked the butter into the flour and rolled out perfect circles, then lifted them easily into pie pans. I offered help, but she said she preferred to have the kitchen to herself. She got me a beer and asked me to keep her company. She talked about four neighbors who were also coming to share the salmon. One, she said, was "a fisherman by profession, but he really likes to spend time in the woods. Real strong and rough, but as sweet and gentle as they come. Real quiet type, you know, never brags, but powerful. And a character: last year he killed a deer by kicking it."

"He did what?" I said, swallowing a little beer down the wrong pipe, and coughing and gasping for breath.

Sherrie had been peeling some fresh peaches for a peach crisp (yes, berry pie *and* peach crisp). She paused in her narrative as she rinsed the knife. She seemed to savor telling me about *Deer Killer.*

"He was driving his motorcycle through the woods and a deer jumped out in front of him. He swerved and missed it so as not to damage his bike, but stuck out his leg and kicked it. Brought the meat over and we butchered it for him. He gave us half."

She put the food on the table as it came out of the oven, with no official dinner hour. The children wandered in, ate what they wanted, then played in the living room. The men arrived. Talked. Sat awhile. Ate whatever was on the table at the moment. Drank beer. Walked outside. Came back in. Ate something else. Drank more beer. The whole time the rock-and-roll played, the children shrieked, and both parents howled at them to pipe down.

I said to Deer Killer, "Heard you kicked a deer to death."

He averted his eyes. "Yeah, guess everybody knows about

that by now. All you can do to keep from hittin' 'em on the roads some years. Sheep ranchers kill the coyotes and mountain lions, you know. Poison 'em. Darn shame. They were here first, you know? Now there's too many deer 'cause there's nothin' left to eat 'em."

Sherrie brought the salmon—broiled with garlic and not overcooked—to the table. I pulled apart the pink, moist flesh with my fork. Fresh salad crunched delightfully in my mouth, sending vinegary dressing flavors to my nose. The berry pie, hot from the oven, with no cornstarch and light on the sugar, ran in tart black streams on my plate. It was a meal fit for royalty, served by a barefoot woman and eaten with no ceremony.

The boom box was still blasting, the kitchen a mess, the adults still talking when I left the gathering for the quiet shelter of my tent. Cacho stood sleeping, tied to an apple tree, when I zipped up my rain fly and fell into a sated slumber.

* * *

The next day Cacho and I descended into the wide, pastoral valley of the Mattole River, parallel to the coast but a few miles inland, separated from the coast by the Cooskie range. To the east stood the taller Rainbow Ridge. Since there was no traffic, I let Cacho take the middle of the street. The road looped up a gentle incline. I relaxed in the saddle, with my arms folded, the reins resting loosely, unattended, on Cacho's neck. He bore me steadfastly on, his steel shoes clacking on the asphalt. To the left an embankment rose ten or twenty feet, topped by some brambles and a dark shape that I assumed was a steer. The motion of the shape did not register in my mind; it kindled no instinctive feelings of caution. A gentle breeze fluffed the hair on that side of my head, threatening to dislodge my hat, and bringing the scent of the animal to Cacho.

The next thing I knew, Cacho was running in the opposite direction—*downhill* on asphalt. It was very sudden. Sparks literally flew from his hooves as we skittered down the road, the reins flapping loosely on his neck. Responding quickly, I pulled on one rein and circled him around until he stopped, facing back toward where the creature lumbered among the briars. Cacho snorted aggressively. The dark shape continued moving slowly and deliberately, apparently unaware of the commotion it had caused. We hadn't bolted far. I could see the animal quite well. As I watched its heavy movements, I realized it was not a steer at all. It was a bear, a black bear.

The bear posed no threat, I knew, but Cacho, with his ranching background, may have had an encounter with a problem bear, or perhaps he had an instinctive fear. He danced nervously.

"Well, Cacho," I spoke aloud, trying to sound calming, "you knew something I didn't, didn't you? You knew it was a bear. Attaboy. It's OK now. Look. See? He doesn't even care about us. He's just doing his thing. It's nothing. Just a little black bear looking for berries. Now, I want you to walk on back up this road, no silliness."

Cacho's body language said, "Nothing doing. That is a bear, and bears are dangerous. Let's go back the way we came."

I needed to behave like a dominant horse in the herd, but I didn't have the teeth for it. Instead, I gave him a sharp wallop on the buttocks with the thick lead rope. He started at the sting and began a jittery little sideways trot.

"No," I said, evenly, collecting the reins and pulling his head in. He tried to turn away from the bear again, but I checked him with the reins. "Just walk. We are just going to walk right on by." I flexed the muscles in my jaw, resolute. Though his motion resembled more of a prance than a walk, Cacho moved at the speed of a walk, and I couldn't really ask for much more. When we were past the bear, Cacho lowered his head and resumed his steady, slow gait. What was beyond sight and scent left no lasting impression on his uncluttered mind.

We passed over a shady, forested rise and down into a pretty valley, cleared of trees but abundant in tall grasses. It was an ecological disaster, featuring exotic plants that provided little habitat for native wildlife, but the flocks of sheep scattered through the pastures found it to their liking. I dismounted to open the gate of a large pasture, then rode up a long driveway. A grand, spreading oak dominated the dry, golden annual grasses.

My sheep ranching hosts greeted me warmly, "Welcome, Lisa, glad you made it." It had been a few days since I had driven through and stopped to talk with them, but they had not forgotten that they had agreed to let me camp. "Make yourself and your horse at home. There's an empty corral on the other side of the barn you can use for him. Listen, honey, why don't you join us for dinner? We'd really love to have you. I insist. Come on up to the house after you get your horse settled in."

"Beautiful spot you've got here," I commented as my hostess prepared the meal.

"Yes, but it is hard to keep the garden nice with all the insects. We sprayed a month ago with Malathion. What a mistake. We're still weak from it, but we're better. We both felt terrible, and our dog is still real sick. He got the worst of it, you know, being out on the lawn and everything. We're sure it was the Malathion and we'll sure never do that again.

Learned our lesson, but, you know, Honey, in some areas they spray that stuff from the air sometimes when there is a Medfly problem. And you can not tell me that doesn't have an effect on people."

"Nice-looking sheep in the pens," I commented after a pause, scratching at the foil at the top of a beer bottle.

"Thanks. We don't have many, really. Just enough to keep him busy." She nodded toward her husband in the family room without looking that way. "We're retired now, been here our whole lives. Ranchers first came here in the late 1800s. It was really very conservative around here in those days, not like now. Country, you know. But in the 1960s a lot of liberal young people came here. Hippies, really, wanting to be closer to nature and, well, of course, grow marijuana." Ranchers had eventually become comfortable with the strange blend of liberal and "redneck" values in the region. They learned to tolerate marijuana growing. "Don't really do no harm. Yes, it's harmless enough. Now, I'm not talking about the bush people. They're another story."

"I've never heard the term." I drew a blank. She asked me to invite her husband to the table, then resumed her story.

"Bush people have little places, less than twenty acres, and they deal in heavier drugs. That's where the trouble is. They have guns, I mean serious weapons and, well, they just aren't the sort of people you want in your community. They're trouble. But the ones that just grow a little marijuana—well, you can't blame people, really. It's easy to grow and very good money. One year not long ago we decided we'd try it," my hostess said, her face reddening. "You know, everyone else around here grows marijuana, so we thought, why not? You can get up to three pounds from one plant, and you can make over $10,000 per plant.

Five or six large plants can net you over $50,000. We weren't greedy; we just wanted to try to grow a few, so we put five plants in the yard."

(This happened more than a dozen years ago, and is probably not a secret, but I think I'll refer to this couple as sheep ranchers rather than using their names. If someone who knows them actually reads what I have written, I wouldn't want their brush with this illegal endeavor to cause them any embarrassment.)

"They grew very well here," her husband interjected as he scooped a helping of fluffy mashed potatoes onto his plate.

"Have some more broccoli." My hostess passed the dish over and continued. "You know, honey, they say marijuana smells skunky, but it doesn't at all. They were such nice plants. Very pretty flowers. We were so close to harvesting when our neighbors turned us in! Can you imagine? And their son deals in the stuff. I mean, really deals in it, not just a couple of plants in the backyard. And other drugs, too. I just don't understand it. Another thing that doesn't make sense: they had won the Lotto last year. Doesn't seem right someone who would do such a mean thing as to turn on a neighbor should win. Honey, take a little more fruit salad. It was a quarter of a million dollars! Doesn't seem like people like that ought to have all the good luck, you know what I mean?"

I voiced my opinion that money had little to do with happiness. My hostess nodded, but didn't seem moved. She looked at her plate and cut her pork chop thoughtfully. "Right after they turned us in, he was caught dealing and had to go to prison. I mean, it's a terrible thing. I'm sorry he had to go to prison." It occurred to her the events might be related, and she brightened up, thinking perhaps there was justice after all.

"Did you end up getting caught?" I asked, forking some macaroni salad.

"No, we cut them down and buried them before anyone got here. It's a small town, you know, dear." She winked at me.

Her husband changed the subject. "How was your day? Did you have a nice ride?"

I said I had, and discussed the bucolic scenery and the good weather. I mentioned I had seen a bear, and laughed about Cacho's sudden reaction. My hosts didn't smile, and asked intently where, exactly, had I seen the bear. I described the spot, and the sheep rancher nodded and said he had heard of a bear roaming that area. Reading the deadly meaning in his eyes, I realized I had done the bear no favors by pinpointing its location.

* * *

One of the things that impressed me was the diversity of philosophies I encountered. People who would have been at odds with each other had in common a willingness to be generous with me. Hospitality flowed my way from a wide assortment of characters. Some were more naturally giving than were others. My next host was the most reluctant benefactor to allow me quarter on his property. Grudging does not begin to describe it. Trying to wring a smile or a sense of welcome out of him was harder than spreading chilled butter on cold pancakes.

The day's ride had been through pleasing rural countryside, ending at his old, two-story, pale canary yellow wooden house. The jowly old man lurked in the shadows inside. His wrinkled, jaundiced skin sagged, and even the clothes surrounding his corpulent, stooped body were faded. The spark of life sputtered dully in him, emitting no light. He had seemed barely able to understand my request when I had driven through a few days earlier, asking if I could camp in his yard. Eventually he had, in his crusty manner, said that I could. When Cacho and I arrived, I spied him though the beveled glass and knocked loudly. He either didn't hear or didn't care, and never came to the door.

I shrugged, and set up camp in his front yard, tying Cacho to a prodigious pear tree. A scratching sound from the other side of the white wooden fence separating the front yard from a well-tended vegetable garden distracted me. I got up and stretched on my tiptoes to see over the fence. I stared in horror. The old man had set a snare and caught a gray squirrel. I described the scene in my journal:

> I couldn't bear to look at the squirrel. He was dan-gling by the neck from a trap—rigged so that it suspended him three feet off the ground. His human-like fingers worked frantically and he kicked and struggled. His bulging eyes seemed to plead for rescue.

I went to the house to tell the old man. I thought I had better play it low-key if the squirrel was to have any chance. I knocked insistently, and the old man answered the call reluctantly. Trying to act casual, I told him about the squir-rel, suggesting that perhaps I could take the little creature down for him. "Let him hang there," he sneered, and slammed the door.

I was aghast that someone would prefer to let an animal suffer. What could I do? It was his property. The death of one gray squirrel would certainly not be the biggest calam-ity the ecology of the region had ever known. My problem was not with the death of the creature, but the suffering troubled me greatly. I felt helpless to intercede, being a barely tolerated visitor, so I returned to Cacho and tried futilely not to think about it.

Eventually the little sounds on the other side of the fence ceased. Greatly relieved it was over, I silently wished the squirrel a good night.

＊
＊ ＊

The next day began pleasantly, the weather mild, but then the road crested and a cold, blustery ocean blast hit my face; the temperature dropped several bone-chilling degrees. The road ran along the beach, with cattle pastures to the east. One or two lazy cattle strolled slowly, stiff-legged across the road, but most of them were lying down in the grass, hugging the ground to try to keep out of the hostile weather. The wind whipped the surf, and the noise of the crashing waves beat like the crescendo of a Beethoven concerto. Cacho fell into a foul mood and hung his head dismally. In an effort to keep myself warm, I led him.

Cacho and I approached a herd of cows clustered on a windswept slope. They were lying with their bony hips to the wind, which blew from our direction. The cow nearest us picked up her head and swiveled her ears, nervous about our approach. As we came nearer, she decided she had better stand, which she did, hindquarters first. Once the first cow stood, the rest followed, so Cacho and I got the full buttocks greeting from the entire herd. I put my gloved hand to my mouth and giggled at their mooning. Cacho held his head low and his ears at a disgruntled angle, indicating he was in no mood for humor.

In early afternoon we arrived at a beautiful ranch settled

against a slope and protected from the ocean breeze. Cacho's attitude improved significantly as he trimmed the lawn.

A young couple, Rick and Janis, tended the property for an absentee owner. They had recently married, and Janis told me about the day. It seemed unremarkable to her that they rode uneventfully down the aisle on horseback. I tried to picture my city friends including any sort of animal in their matrimonial ceremony, and came up only with humorous, chaotic scenarios involving splashes of animal urine on white satin shoes, or crashing tables with tumbling wedding cakes and telltale frosting on untrimmed whiskers.

As Janis and I chatted, Rick came out of the house, adjusted the brim of his baseball cap and said, "Lisa, some friends of ours are coming over to spend the night and we're going to round up two of the cows this evening. Need to take a look at them 'cause they haven't been doing too good. Anyway, I was thinking, would you like to come with us? You know, see the ranch. You can ride your horse if you want, or you can give him a rest and ride on the quad runner with me."

I rode on the back of the quad runner, a little, four-wheel, motorcycle-type vehicle. We covered ground more quickly on the ORV than the three horses could, so he and I did the initial survey of the herd to find the two sick cows. I shared an uncomfortable plywood platform with a cow dog. The three of us bounced along, swinging wide around the herd, bringing the animals back to where the three equestrians would meet us and help drive the two sick ones to a squeeze chute. I gripped the lip of the plywood behind me, trying to stay on and help the dog stay on while we dipped and careened through the pastures. Even my unpadded McClellan saddle would have seemed like a Naugahyde Easy-Boy lounger compared to this hard, bouncing perch. The ORV threatened to overturn as we raced along steep slopes and through sodden marshes.

As if driving nothing more challenging than a tour bus, the young rancher narrated as we worked. "Cape Ranch," he shouted over the engine and the wind, "is located in the most western part of the continental United States." The landscape reveled in its lonely desolation, wind-scoured and denuded of scrub, yet rich in grasses that blanketed the rolling hills on the coastal outcrop. Pulling a veil of misty coastal layer across its face, the sun blushed crimson, giving the pasture a soft glow.

We found a small herd that included the two cows that had infected eyes. The dog jumped down eagerly, barking and nipping at the cows' legs with little effect. "Cancer eye," Rick informed me. "It's real far along. Maybe I should have gathered them up sooner, but it stresses 'em every time you mess with 'em. Better to leave 'em alone. Oh, look. Here come the horses. Now we can separate 'em out."

Rick's mare, ridden by his friend, spent a lot of time and energy crow-hopping and rearing. Eventually, after the bunch with the sick cows had scattered and been collected a couple of times—a few of the cows drifting away each time—only four, including the two that needed treatment, remained. Three equestrians and one dog surrounded the nervous beasts, trying to get them to go through a gate in the pipe-rail corral. The edgy cows breathed heavily, looking for an out. One of the cows with a bad eye made a run for it and escaped, dodging past the bucking mare.

"It's too far gone, anyway; she's gonna lose the eye. Just get this one!" Rick yelled. The cow dog barked and the horses pranced, but with only one cow to watch, they got her in. She bolted in wildly, bruising her hip with a crunch against the gate.

Rick turned off the noisy engine of the quad runner and ran to help. Janis leaned down from the saddle and slammed the gate shut behind the cow, then quickly pulled the lever on the squeeze chute, bringing metal bars in from both sides to hold the cow's body tightly. The cow struggled initially but then relaxed. Rick, his feet spread wide in case she resisted, grabbed her head and twisted it, holding her in a neck lock so he could get a good look at her.

Disease had ruptured her eye, and she had several teeth missing. Life for her would be an agonizing, day-to-day battle for survival. "She has a good calf," Rick told me, so he sprayed her face with Furazone and let her go rather than destroying her. She trotted off toward the other cows as if somehow trying to regain her dignity, her movements not betraying her chronic discomfort.

6

Reaching a Conclusion

*A*fter camping in a barn at Cape Ranch, I spent two days in Ferndale, its Victorian architecture adorned with intricate paint jobs. Pastel lavender and blue, bold burgundy and black, hot pink and mint green; all sorts of imaginative color combinations enhanced the detailed woodwork. As if to emphasize contrasts, the next three days took me through beautiful physical surroundings, but with nondescript architecture.

North of Arcata, I arrived at a campground called Clam Beach. Though I was tired and hungry, I took a moment to visit the beach and let Cacho step in the waves, which he found eternally fascinating. I had time to consider my fellow visitors to the park. There could not have been two more disparate groups of people. Well-groomed urbanites driving new, recently washed SUVs contrasted with bedraggled transients, some with no motor transportation at all, but those with wheels drove and lived in leftover models from the 1960s that had, to all appearances, not been cleaned since then. I noted that the people with good hygiene were only "day-use visitors" and that the more earthy community would be my companions for the night. Not being free of bias, this understanding made me uneasy.

The beach park included picnic facilities and enclosures for horses, though Cacho was the only equine visitor. A man with a graying beard and a frayed GRATEFUL DEAD sweatshirt sat among his camping gear near the best stall. He was missing one leg, which made me self-conscious. Because he camped so close to the stall, I thought he might consider it part of his territory. Overcoming my unease, I cleared my throat and awkwardly asked permission to use it. He answered pleasantly, showing me a measure of his stained, broadly spaced teeth.

A fourth set of shoes near Arcata — Photo by Lisa Wood

"Horses have the right of way in McKinleyville."
"Well, that's nice of you, but you were here first—"
"No, it's no trouble. I don't need the stall. Hey, I like

having a horse nearby." He chatted a bit about horses; told me he had one himself when he was a kid. Also, he told me about losing his leg in a motorcycle accident. Despite my preconception, he put me at ease. I decided he would make a fine neighbor for Cacho.

I searched through the fifty-five-gallon barrels provided for litter, looking for a plastic container I could modify with my knife to make a watering container for Cacho. I had been finding clean, empty water containers at previous campsites, but this time my luck ran out. There were water faucets near the picnic tables, and the gravel under them wasn't draining well, so I started filling one of the gravel-bottom rings with water, holding Cacho by his halter rope with my other hand.

The dirtiest, scariest-looking man at the park wandered over. My heart skipped a beat when I realized he was approaching me. Sunken eyes and gaunt cheeks suggested he hadn't eaten well in weeks. His threadbare jacket looked as if it wasn't enough to keep him comfortable in the afternoon breeze. An old, faded red bandanna, dark with grime, kept his stringy gray hair out of his face.

"You gonna let your horse drink that?" His thin, chapped lips moved slowly, an unreadable look on his face. A moist pink conjunctiva surrounded his dull gray irises.

"I was planning to," I said, trying to sound casual.

"Don't people do their dishes in there? I mean, isn't there soap and crap in there?" The pace of his speech picked up and his eyes narrowed, seeming to focus more clearly.

I had a piercing realization that he had no evil intent; he only wanted to help. It flooded my soul with shame for my rude judgement based on his appearance. Even appreciating his goodwill, I reflexively insisted I was OK. I didn't need his help. I answered, "Yeah, I think so, but I think plenty of water washes through and it's OK just this once."

"Wait a minute," he said, with what seemed like uncustomary enthusiasm. He rummaged in his belongings and came back with a rectangular plastic container suitable for giving Cacho a drink. "Try this," he said, rinsing it out and then filling it up. His mouth curled into a satisfied grin as Cacho obligingly took a long drink. "I used to own a horse," he explained. His voice suggested that some fondly remembered, long-past time had surfaced in his mind. He looked briefly at me, then back at Cacho, and said, "Nice horse. Keep the container till you leave. Just leave it there by my stuff when you go." He tramped away, with almost a swagger in his step.

﹡ ﹡ ﹡

Once Cacho was taken care of, I set up my own camp near the picnic tables. A clean, new burgundy-colored van pulled into the nearby lot. A tall, handsome, swarthy man helped an elderly couple and a boy about six years old to get out. The man spoke to the older couple in a language I couldn't place. He spoke to the boy in unaccented English. The boy spoke only English.

The man plunked an ice chest onto a picnic table near me. The small, stooped old woman, her thin fingers slightly gnarled from arthritis, began removing eggs, fresh, ripe tomatoes, golden-brown onions, and other delicious-looking foods. She wore a serious expression, and looked down her substantial nose at her task, apparently without need of glasses. The elderly man brought out a Coleman stove and began preparing it, while the younger man threw a ball with the boy.

My mouth watered as the onions began to cook, filling the cool salty air with the promise of rich flavors. I quickly made a dehydrated meal of beef stew, and casually carried it over to where the man and the boy were playing. "Afternoon," I said. "Bit windy."

"Yes, but it looks as if the sun may finally be coming out." The man responded. "You traveling by horseback?"

"Uh-huh."

"How far are you going?"

When I told him, he became enthusiastic about my adventure and called his son over to learn about survival matters. "This lady is spending more than three months camping. What do you think she packed with her?"

As I was planning this trip, my friends, concerned about my safety, had consulted the Fear-mongers Catalogue and developed long lists of recommended gear. Equipment does provide a degree of safety and, in some cases, comfort, but if I were to take all of the "essential" provisions suggested, I would need a twenty-mule team to carry them. In the end I boiled it down to three things that one should carry—well, four, if you count duct tape: *determination; resourcefulness; and a good sense of humor.*

These were the only tools that would do me any good in those completely unpredictable situations that inevitably happen. Certainly there were some basics that I needed: extra rope, a knife, cook stove and matches, tent, topical antiseptic, sleeping bag, canteen, water purifier and food. Really, that's about it.

I brought a lot more, much of which I had discarded along the way, such as a cow bell and vet wrap. I hadn't used the water purifier, nor the easy boots (rubber horse booties) I carried in case Cacho threw a shoe while we were away from phones and access to farriers. I brought rock salt, though on the salty coast Cacho didn't need it. The hatchet, collapsible saw, pliers, wire-cutters, and compass saw little action.

I expected the boy to think of superfluous items, such as a cellular phone, Walkman, etc., but I underestimated his practicality. His long lashes hid serious brown eyes, and he kept his head down bashfully, but he quickly listed most of the essentials—sleeping bag, rain jacket, tent and flashlight.

I nodded to indicate he had answered well. "Food," I added, sensing my opening, smelling the onions beginning to brown as the old woman attended to dinner. "But dehydrated food leaves a little to be desired." I tipped my pot so that he could see in. The boy made a face. The swarthy man rewarded me with an invitation to dinner. I doubted the two less wholesome-looking men I had interacted with earlier would have received such a warm offer, if they had made themselves available as I had.

As we assembled at the table, we continued the gear game.

"What else?" the father prompted, but the boy seemed to have lost interest.

"Canteen," I suggested, "and a toothbrush."

"A toothbrush!" the swarthy man exclaimed, "Do you really need that?"

"Well," I said, "perhaps it's not absolutely essential to survival, at least not in the short run, but it doesn't weigh much."

After teasing me for a bit, the man admitted that he was a dentist. I laughed. "I even packed a little tube of toothpaste," I said, but admitted sheepishly, "I didn't bring any dental floss."

He said he was from Iran, and that his parents spoke only Farsi. He translated for them. The small, wiry older people smiled and nodded and exchanged a few words. "They say your trip is a good idea." By the amused looks on their faces, he clearly took liberties with the translation.

After eating, the family packed up and prepared to leave. "We just came for dinner," the dentist explained. I gave him a very broad view of my teeth, saying, "I surely did enjoy your company, and of course the food."

The dentist turned his attention to loading his family into the van, but as he steered out of the parking lot he pulled to the curb by my campsite. He rolled down his window and beckoned. He handed me a roll of dental floss. "A little present for you."

One by one, all the nice clean cars followed the dentist, leaving me in the company of the ragged men. We all retreated inside our tents and campers to escape the cold, wet night air.

* * *

Over the months of travel, I had pitched my tent under a vast variety of trees, on beaches, in meadows, in gullies and on porches. I found the occasional barn a high-ceilinged treat. Occasionally, a kind soul offered a soft bed, and three hotels were able to accommodate both horse and rider. Two days' ride from Clam Beach, I slept in a horse trailer—a singular event, and surprisingly enjoyable.

I had been given permission to camp at Redwood RV Park, where RVs and cars with tents and Coleman stoves packed the rows of small spaces. People strode busily around the grounds to the bathrooms and the convenience store. Squeezing Cacho into one of the little RV spaces would attract attention, which would not be relaxing. I surveyed the scene with distaste, then cast about for a more horse-friendly alternative. The stable manager agreed to let me use one of the corrals.

I looked for a suitable nearby place for my tent. The grassy spot between two horse trailers looked good. As I walked over, the gray clouds began to release a silent, soft mist of rain. On impulse, I stepped into one of the trailers. Leather gear and manure was strewn all over the floor. It was a "gooseneck" trailer, and the platform above the pickup bed was relatively clear of gear. If I slept there I would not have to pack up my wet tent in the morning, and could perhaps continue to avoid the nauseating smell of mildew. I pulled a couple of bridles out of the way and spread out my sleeping bag on the dusty metal.

I fell asleep quickly. An hour or two later I awoke to hear the soft tapping of light rain on my metal roof. I sat up as far as I could without hitting my head and looked out at the blackness, smelled the fresh, cool wetness through the rank odor of gear and manure in the trailer, and nestled back into my warm bag, feeling the cold, hard metal under me. There was no bite of wind, just sweet rain, which shifted from mist to rain and back to mist again during the night, wetting the ground evenly.

In the dim light of dawn I saddled Cacho, the moisture darkening the saddle leather. My slicker kept me comfortable as I traveled the old highway, just east of the current thoroughfare. Cacho chose the center of the deserted road, which tunneled its way through hemlocks, spruces and redwoods. In J. Smeaton Chase's book, which had inspired me to undertake this journey, he described it as a "superb forest," and he did not exaggerate. The black soil supported a rich carpet of ferns, mushrooms and mosses. A straight line of tiny quail followed their stiffly erect mother as she hurried from beneath some bushes and across the pavement. The road circled around the east side of a very still pond, "Freshwater Lagoon," and the trees on the surrounding hillsides reflected in the mirror-like surface blemished only by floating leaves. Two large black vultures soared majestically overhead. Here and there a driveway to a house diverged from the road, and one particularly grand mansion reached down to the shore of the pond.

I observed a sedan parked on the roadside. As I neared, I noted heavy condensation on the inside of the windows. The rim around the license plate identified the car as a rental. Cacho brought me steadily nearer, and finally I saw two young, blond women and one brunette sprawled on the seats inside, snoring deeply, in a tangle of legs, arms and hair. Bits of debris—food wrappers and clothing—were strewn all over the interior of the car, and a half-eaten loaf of bread and some fruit warmed under the back window. I tipped my hat to the unconscious travelers and wished them sweet dreams and a *bon voyage*.

As the road joined the highway, heavy traffic jolted me from my pleasant daydreaming. Log trucks thundered by, but I felt that I had already bested the behemoths, so I scarcely paid them any mind.

In Orick, a flock of vendors hawked their redwood carvings along the side of the road. Oceans of carved whales and polyurethane-coated burl coffee table tops jutted from roadside yards. Large letters advertised best prices. It was reminiscent of a garage sale or a Third-World bazaar. Though probably handmade, the wooden whales, bears, busts and eagles had a mass-produced feeling.

Just past town, in Elk Prairie, several cars had pulled off the side road, and tourists snapped photos of a herd of elk. The large, majestic animals posed in a vast meadow bearing their name. They appeared to pay no attention to the photographers, but their disdain seemed false, as I noticed that the graceful animals were evidently aware of the people, since they casually kept their distance. Or, perhaps it was not an act. Perhaps they knew their power only too well, and chose to avoid the photo frenzy out of aloofness, not fear. After all, they were tall, intimidating animals, able to deflect a mountain lion with a flick of a hoof. I thought of the damage those impressive horns could do to delicate human flesh. Past the throng of tourists, a large male elk stepped out of some roadside bushes. His muscles rippled in a self-confident trot that took him not more than ten feet from us, then across the road where he disappeared again into the underbrush. I patted Cacho's neck, grateful that he was less stunned by the event than was I.

* * *

The next day took us to the south bank of the Klamath River, where we entered the Yurok Indian Reservation. I didn't expect anything to be different because of this designation. My intent in selecting this destination had been a preoccupation with the long, unavoidable span of bridge crossing the river. Since a nervous horse will spook blindly, as Cacho had when he saw the bear, bridges with traffic on one side and a deadly chasm over the edge posed a double hazard. My plan was to get to sleep early so I could cross the bridge before traffic picked up.

The "Indian RV Park" consisted of a grassy field with a row of hookups nestled on the south bank of the Klamath. A handful of trailers and campers were irregularly spaced among the many available slots. I chose a spot at the end nearest the river. Using my cook pot, I rinsed Cacho's back. The spigot leaked badly and sprayed water, effectively showering me as well. A man in a fishing hat and leisure wear emerged from one of the trailers. Robert was in his late seventies, but looked younger.

"Ah, you made it!" Robert greeted me. He unlocked the metal storage shed where he had put my hay, and loaned me a bucket for watering Cacho. "She's here, Hon," he yelled at his wife, Helen. They invited me to join them for some Select Cola, a popular brand in this area. We settled ourselves in white plastic chairs, with Cacho nearby, his neck stretching to the lush grass.

"The Indian who owns the place, I told him I said it was OK for you to stay here. He isn't always around, but he's here today. He may charge you a little something for spending the night." Robert fidgeted uncomfortably as we discussed financial matters.

"That's fine with me. I'm perfectly happy to pay," I said, and Robert looked relieved. "Beautiful spot here, right on the river," I added.

"Yes, we like it. Hear the water? Sounds nice don't it? Some good fishing in that river. Hey, do you like salmon? We canned the last one I got. I'll get some for you."

"I'll get it, dear." Helen rose in a smooth motion, no sign of old-age infirmities. She disappeared into the trailer, reappearing shortly bearing a glass jar. I opened the jar and used my fingers to dig the delectable fishy contents out of the oily brine.

"Delicious!" I proclaimed, licking my glistening fingers.

"Caught that one right over there." Robert pointed toward the mighty river.

A red pickup turned into the campground and parked at the far end. "That's the owner. He'll probably come down here to collect his fee." Sure enough, the thin, dark man made his way over. His legs wobbled, and I surmised he'd been drinking. He asked me for some money, and then he and Robert wandered off to discuss some plumbing problems.

Helen said, "He lets us pretty much run the place. That's his dog over there; his name is Bear." She pointed with her chin toward a big white dog that was chasing birds in the meadow. "The Indians don't take too good care of their dogs, but this one's tough." As she talked, a petite woman with long black hair came out of a small building and ran timidly toward another building, hotly pursued by the dog. Bear seemed to think it a jolly game, and barked playfully to encourage her. "That's his wife. She's afraid of dogs," Helen added.

Cacho, having eaten quite a bit, made a large pile of manure near where we sat. "I'll clean up after him in the morning," I said, my turn to be embarrassed.

"Oh, don't you worry. We'll take care of that. It's good to have you here. Your trip sounds so exciting."

Bear, tired of chasing the woman, came over to see the horse. Bear found Cacho placid and boring, but the pile of moist, fresh manure interested him greatly. Bear rolled in it, then, for extra doggy measure, ate some. He shook vigorously, showing off the green streaks on his pale coat.

Robert and the proprietor turned from their discussion and walked back to where my hostess and I sat in the plastic chairs. "That's my dog," the owner slurred. "He's the Horse Shit Dog." He thought that was pretty funny, and staggered away, stuttering loudly, "Yessir! Come on, Horse Shit Dog!" eliminating all doubts about his sobriety.

As planned, I got up early the next morning, before the sun had a chance to make an impression on the temperature. I faced the long, narrow bridge across the powerful, fast-flowing river. "All right, buddy, let's just saddle up and go, OK? You can graze when we get to the other side. This is a big, wide river, and that bridge is going to be nasty if the logging trucks go booming across while we're on it."

Thanks to Cacho's calm nature, the whole bridge crossing was rather anticlimactic. I'd like to believe my planning had something to do with it, but it was probably just another day in the life of my four-legged guardian angel. While we were on the bridge, only one car crossed, and it had plenty of room to get around us.

* ⋆ *

Two nights later, with clouds threatening a major storm, I paid a small fee at the Crescent City fairground, and had my choice of stalls in the long, metal-roofed barns. I found several clean compartments with fresh piles of sawdust ready to be spread as bedding. I dumped the gear in a gloomy compartment. The blue-black sky darkened while I took Cacho on a tour of the fairgrounds.

In a small, round arena a woman rode a large, flea-bitten Arabian gelding in circles. She had a vise-like grip on her four reins, pulling hard to keep the animal collected. She looked quite grim, making riding look like grueling work.

In stark contrast, nearby, a thin man with delicate hands unloaded two handsome, dark mules from a very nice rig with dual wheels and running lights. The license plate read, MULE LUV. The plate's frame read, "I get my kicks from mules." Gently, he led his neatly groomed animals to their stalls.

The woman who had been riding jerked on the rope as she led the horse past us, and then struggled to get him into a stall, whipping the animal's neck with a length of thin leather and yanking on his halter. The halter was fitted with a chain to inflict pain on the top of the nose when tugged. The more she pulled, the more agitated her horse became and the more he resisted. The woman yelled and cursed at him, and even after he was in his stall she gave him a couple of whacks with the leather strap out of anger and frustration. As she jerked his halter off, he threw his head up, trying to get out of her reach. I felt as if I had witnessed a crime, and slithered away before I could be caught.

Seated at a picnic table with Cacho grazing nearby, I finished reading *Catch-22,* though my mind wasn't on it. I was troubled by the unnecessary violence I had seen. I put the book down and looked at Cacho, who could patiently listen better than any paid psychologist. "I hate that," I confided. "I hate it when people take out their aggressions on a helpless animal. Why have a horse if it doesn't bring you pleasure?" Cacho flicked an ear in my direction, a calm, wise look in his eyes as he thoughtfully munched grass. "Those mules, the guy who had the mules, that's the way it should be." A piece of grass tickled Cacho's chin, and he nodded his head in agreement.

At that very moment, as if commenting on the issue, the heavy clouds suddenly released an invigorating rain. Water ran in rivulets down Cacho's furry sides. "Better put you up before you get soaked and too cold, eh?"

John Muir said, "The winds will blow their own freshness into you, and the storms their energy, while cares will drop off like autumn leaves." For me, that is true. My vexation regarding the treatment of the horse was washed away as we splashed through the exhilarating rain. Cacho retreated happily into a secure barn stall, but I wasn't tired yet. Heavy streams of water spanked the ground noisily as I moved down the length of both barns, greeting each of the occupants. In appreciation of my gentle touch, the flea-bitten Arab blew hot breath on my palm with his big, fuzzy, nostrils. I scratched his forelock and he put his head down so I could reach him better.

Finally, I crawled into my sleeping bag on a nest of clean sawdust, listening to the rain on the metal roof and the distant rumble of thunder. As the thunder grew louder, horses shifted nervously in their stalls. Electricity sizzled through the rain-freshened air. Brilliant light flashed, and a deafening crack followed soon after. The horse on the other side of the wall from me kicked his stall walls, and pranced and snorted nervously. I checked on Cacho, who slept peacefully. As I snuggled back to bed, the steady drumming and splashing of water carried me to sweet barn dreams.

The storm spent its fury by the time a soft light crept through the open half of the stall door, and only a faint growl of thunder resonated from the distant misty mountains. The rain, however, continued at a steady, light drizzle through the day.

As I approached Smith River, the northernmost town in California, the rain began to fall in earnest. The wind changed direction and blew cold. A hawk glared at me from a fence post, his wings hunched against the weather. I hurried to my accommodations, where two horses ran to the barbed wire to greet Cacho. Along the drive, magnificent lilies shuddered under the pelting raindrops. Just past the blossoms, I unsaddled Cacho near a large shed, open on one side, which housed a tractor and other pieces of equipment. As I piled my gear under the overhang, my hostess, Pat, emerged from her house with a friendly wave and matter-of-fact attitude.

The thin woman with neatly trimmed gray hair introduced Cacho to a large pasture with plenty of grass and a few Angus cattle. Although a little goat had dominated Cacho a few weeks earlier, he had no trouble keeping the large steers at bay while he ate. He laid his ears back and occasionally swung his head around and bared his teeth. Pat's horses worried the fence line of their enclosure, trying to get his attention, but he ignored them entirely.

At first, Pat looked like a serious, maybe even an unhappy,

person. This impression came from her habit of setting her thin-lipped mouth firmly in a frowning position. She spoke between frowns. I soon found, however, that my conclusion had been premature. This sixty-something woman, with liver spots on her hands to attest to her outdoor life, had, in contrast to her appearance, a youthful exuberance. Even more remarkable was her habit of trivializing her own difficulties, and of making her ministrations to others seem no effort at all.

She brought me into her house, and introduced me to her small dogs and her two cats. While I showered, she made a big batch of spaghetti sauce and cooked some cow bones for the dogs. I emerged from the steamy bathroom to a house filled with the savory aromas of onion and garlic. I joined her in the kitchen. Noticing the cow magnet and cow oven mitt, I observed, "You like cows?"

"Love them. Jersey cows especially. The saying goes, 'On the first day, God created the Jersey ... and it was all downhill from there.'" I had to agree that the soft, ginger Jerseys had the gentlest, brownest eyes of any animal I had ever seen.

"Almost ready for the big finish, hmm? How do you feel, relieved?"

"Mixed feelings, I guess. It's kinda like reading a book. I don't know about you, but I hurry up reading a book to find out what happens. I'm eager to finish it, but then when I get to the last page, I'm sorry it's over. Tomorrow I turn the last page. I'm kinda looking forward to it, but it also makes me sad, like coming to the end of a good book."

I wrote in my journal, too: "Today is the last day of my journey. I feel healthy, happy and content. The trip has been good for me physically and spiritually. Physically, I have thrived on lots of not-too-strenuous activity, fresh air, and sleeping on the ground. Spiritually, I have gained from a combination of solitude and socializing. People I have met have built up my self-esteem with compliments on my sense of humor, my patience, my ability to make the best of things, my ease as a houseguest, and my courage. Men have flattered me with comments such as, 'There is the woman of my dreams.' Both men and women have told me that I look great—even after a few days without a shower.

"Now, however, I must return home to people who have seen me in moments when I have not been happy, when I have lost my patience, and when I have failed to see the bright side of a situation. My moment in the spotlight is almost over. No men from home have been dreaming about my return. Friends with whom I play volleyball will be interested in a brief summary of my adventure, co-workers will pretend to be interested in my photos, and my cat will want to sit in my lap and purr. However, though my cat will never tire of my lap, special interest in my adventures from humans will fade. My pilgrimage will become nothing but a pleasant memory, one so unlike my day-to-day reality that it might have been nothing but a dream."

* * *

As I rode the last miles on a bright, sunny August day, I reflected on the panic that had choked me on the first day. Time ceased to be linear for me. It seemed that I had seen the entire state in one day.

Dad pulled up with my horse trailer, and Mom arrived in their station wagon, bringing my nephew, Eric, and a teenage friend of the family from Germany. I put Eric, a spindly, seven-year-old sprout with long arms and legs, on Cacho's back while we waited for the hour when I had told friends I would take the last steps across the border. Eric liked sitting on my horse, but soon got down. Normally, having a child around my horse put me into a state of rigid vigilance, but I was relaxed and my guard was down. So of course Cacho accidentally found Eric's little foot and absently stepped on it. Eric screamed as though a lion was mauling him, and Cacho took another leisurely step, releasing Eric from the pressure. An intense examination of the foot revealed no damage.

Friends, including Pat, arrived in the nick of time. Everyone piled out of cars and joined my parade up the road, past the fruit inspection station and into Oregon. With great ceremony, one friend gave me a miniature navy blue Oregon state flag, and, cameras clicking, I posed in front of the WELCOME TO OREGON sign. J. Smeaton Chase had cantered a bit into Oregon, so I did, as well.

At a beach located right on the border, we celebrated with champagne and smoked salmon for the humans, and baby carrots and Budweiser in long-necked bottles—his favorite—for Cacho. Everyone laughed while I held the bottle for Cacho, and the foam dripped down my arm.

As the big, red sun sank toward the sea, I excused myself for one last ride up the beach. In a carefree, exhilarating canter, Cacho obligingly pounded up and down the strand, his mane and tail flying, sharing his strength with me. There on the beach, at the very end of the adventure, he captured for me the image I had been chasing, the dream I had followed so many miles.

A suitable distance away from my friends and family, I dismounted. Cacho stood patiently while I reclined on the beach, reflecting. Aldo Leopold advises us, "Think hard of everything you have seen and tried to understand." I asked myself what I had learned, and how I had changed. I sagged with disappointment in myself for having gone to all this trouble and developed no profound insights.

As the ocean swallowed the sun, I thought about the months that had just slipped by. I had been the guest of many people, and the wilderness had welcomed me too. I had ridden into spectacular vistas and become part of them. I had heard the pulsing harmony of nature. I had some great adventures and met some wonderful, generous people. They had gentled my fall when I jumped from the airplane, and had brought me safely back to the ground, where friends and family waited. I could genuinely say I would never be the same.

I stood up and dusted the sand off my pants. Scratching Cacho's forehead to make him nod, I said, "Well, maybe I learned a little something about the importance of friendship."

Welcome to Oregon — Photo by Chris Donohoe

Celebrating at the Oregon border — Photo by Chris Donohoe

Cacho celebrates — Photo by Julia Carls

More celebrating — Photo by Merle Wood

Lisa takes one last canter — Photo by Julia Carls

Lisa reflects on her journey — Photo by Julia Carls

7

Reaching Back

Upon clicking my heels and returning home, there were many things to enjoy, but first there was enormous grief to overcome. My friends, Susan and Derek, took me to visit Jory in the hospital. He lay motionless in his hospital crib, hooked up to tubes and monitors. His big, bald head held closed, sunken eyes. "They tell us it will be soon. We have to decide if we should take him home to die."

It took several weeks after they brought him home, but he finally stopped breathing one night, soon after Susan had rocked him and told him it was all right with her if he died. He was twenty months old. A friend let us use her boat to scatter his tiny little handful of ashes onto the powerful sea. Crying with my friends was the hardest part of returning to my former life.

At work, I had to learn to live inside again, where the wind never blows and the mists never come, and the light always looks the same. The filtered air in my office provided a constant humidity and the same neutral odor. Never did pungent sage, the rotting miasma of corpses, or refreshing pine overwhelm me as I sat at my computer. No wind blew my hat off, strangling me as it tugged at the keeper around my throat. The air in my office did not move, did not pepper my skin with blown sand, did not caress it with a soft breeze.

Before I started my trip, I had thought I would be lonely without conversation and the constant input from the radio at home and in my car. I hadn't missed these things at all. But when I returned to the city and my indoor life, I missed the sun and stars, the wind, even the fog, and the constant, steady motion that Cacho and I had superimposed on the movement of the waves and the rustling trees. I longed for the sudden scurry of lizards underfoot. Eventually, however, I grew accustomed to the sameness of my house and office and forgot about the things I missed.

City life had its compensations. With appreciation I flipped light switches, illuminating whole rooms with a touch of a finger. I went to my favorite bar and grill in Pacific Beach and had a burger, rare, and it tasted just as good as I remembered. I had been dreaming of that burger for the last couple of weeks. My cat and I slept soundly on my soft bed with clean bedding, but soon I began waiting for a chance to fall asleep reading a book about another adventure, hoping my dreams would lead me in a new direction.

For the moment, my feet were shackled, the wanderlust checked by my own limitations. A pain that had developed in my lower leg toward the end of my adventure had grown worse. I could hardly walk. I called my massage therapist and made an appointment. He thought that all the walking I had done in the last few months had exacerbated an old wound, and that scar tissue had built up.

After an intense massage session I went to bed, and got up in the morning without pain, though I actually didn't notice it was missing. Then, reading the morning paper, I happened to look down at my feet. I called my massage therapist in a panic because my whole foot had swollen into a puffy mess the size of a cantaloupe. He assured me that was normal, just water and junk he had flushed out of my tissues. He must have been correct because over the course of the day the swelling went down. "How is the pain?" he asked. That's when it occurred to me that the pain was gone. It was a rather dramatic, sudden and somewhat miraculous recovery.

The next weekend I drove to the beach to play volleyball. I felt strong and athletic, and that helped compensate for the lack of practice. One friend from the volleyball group, I discovered, had driven to the Oregon border to join the celebration on my last day, but hadn't found us. He was amazingly good-natured about the mix-up.

"Yeah, right. You were staying in a hotel somewhere. You were never even at the border. You never rode anywhere." He teased.

I'm glad I have the photos to prove it wasn't just a dream.